DION FORTUNE & THE LOST SECRETS OF THE WEST

ARTICLES FROM THE
INNER LIGHT JOURNAL 2002-5

GARETH KNIGHT

© Gareth Knight, 2020

This anthology first published in Great Britain in 2020 by Skylight Press,
210 Brooklyn Road, Cheltenham, Glos GL51 8EA

All rights reserved. Except for the quotation of short passages for the purposes of criticism and review, no part of this publication may be reproduced, stored in a retrieval system or transmitted, in any form or by any means, electronic, mechanical, photocopying, recording or otherwise, without the prior consent of the copyright holder and publisher.

Gareth Knight has asserted his right to be identified as the author of this work.

Designed and typeset by Rebsie Fairholm.
Cover photo by Nick/Adobe Stock.
Publisher: Daniel Staniforth.

www.skylightpress.co.uk

Typeset in Adobe Caslon Pro.

British Library Cataloguing in Publication Data.
A catalogue record for this book is available from the British Library.

ISBN 978-1-910098-03-5

CONTENTS

Dion Fortune and the Lost Secrets of the West — 5

The Western Esoteric Tradition and Popular Culture — 27

The Dweller on the Threshold — 47

Journey to the Moon — 60

Fantasy, Belief and Reality — 72

Chrétien de Troyes – The First Arthurian Romancer — 83

The Elemental Tides — 93

Do You Believe in Fairies…? — 103

Dion Fortune and the Mystical Qabalah — 112

Is There a Psychic in the House? — 121

The Magical World of Dion Fortune — 129

The Red Rose and the White — 135

DION FORTUNE AND THE LOST SECRETS OF THE WEST

Talk given by Gareth Knight at the Temenos Academy, 3rd February 2003

SINCE ITS foundation the Temenos Academy has been an impressive forum for showing people the doors of the different sacred traditions, although its remit does not extend to actually taking anyone through them. There are of course many such doors, and having passed through one of them some fifty years ago and lived to tell the tale, it may be helpful if I recount something of what I found there.

The door through which I entered, as a young man of 23, was that of the Society of the Inner Light, founded by Dion Fortune. The force that propelled me through it was my reaction to reading *The Esoteric Orders and their Work*, a book she wrote soon after founding her school. In this I read that "in all ages and among all races there has existed a tradition concerning certain esoteric schools or fraternities, wherein a secret wisdom unknown to the generality of mankind might be learnt, and to which admission was obtained by means of an initiation in which tests and ritual played their part." This acted like a trumpet call for me, and I immediately decided that wherever these words were coming from, that was where I wanted to be.

Well, where were they coming from? Who put them there? And on what authority? These I suppose are modern equivalents to the famous Graal questions, when the signs of the Mysteries are first trailed before the innocent questor. Although another question that

I might well ask myself today is, would I react in quite the same way now? Either in the light of fifty years more life experience, looking back into the 20th century, or if I were coming to it afresh as a young man today with eyes cast forward into the 21st.

Leafing through the pages of *The Esoteric Orders and their Work* today, and its companion volume *The Training and Work of an Initiate*, published in 1928 and 1930 respectively, I find at first glance a number of things that young educated people of today might now find to be stumbling blocks. It includes a rather facile cosmology of the seven planes and great beings of one kind and another that seem taken from elementary Theosophy, together with what appears to be a highly dubious account of ancient history with much emphasis upon emigrations from the lost continent of Atlantis.

On the other hand, I have no regrets about doing what I did in 1953 and enrolling in the school that the author of this book had founded. Had I taken a more sophisticated and worldly wise attitude I might have missed one of the greatest opportunities of my life, which has led to a steady expansion of consciousness and richness of spiritual life over the subsequent fifty years.

During this time I have had to rearrange a fair amount of mental furniture, as one does in the course of life, coming to terms with different levels of appreciation of esoteric tradition, along with increasing depth of understanding. One finds much the same spectrum of realisation in the religious sphere, from the naïve acceptance of the Bible stories to the more complex subtleties of the nature of the divine being and attributes debated by theologians. This does not mean that the child who seeks to sit at the feet of gentle Jesus is any further distant from the truth than the theologian who can descant on the mysteries of the hypostatic union. Indeed we have it on good authority that the way to heaven is considerably easier for the former. So let us not jettison our naïve beliefs too readily. They might come in handy one day.

So let us take a brief look, not only at where Dion Fortune was coming from when she wrote these books that so affected my life, but where she was going to. And thence where I and some others who have shared her vision have arrived as a result of heeding what she said.

Her own first steps upon the Path were not very easy ones, and I suppose they never are for the pioneer. She was born Violet Mary Firth in 1890 in fairly comfortable middle class circumstances. Her father was a solicitor with business interests in a hydrotherapeutic establishment, first in Llandudno, North Wales, where she was born, and then near Weston-super-Mare in Somerset where she spent most of her childhood years. Her parents later moved to London and developed an interest in Christian Science, which their daughter did not particularly share, and then became enthusiasts of the Garden City movement at Letchworth, with its high Utopian ideals in those days.

Violet Mary Firth was a bright imaginative child who at the age of sixteen had some early verse and her photograph printed in a national magazine, *The Girls' Realm*. An early but by no means remarkable indication of her later power with the pen. Her adult ambitions were more practical, for at about the age of twenty she went to college to study horticulture, which at the time was being developed as a possible avenue for young women who sought some kind of profession to follow, in an era when there was very little opportunity for them, educational or vocational. She completed a two year course and was about to be taken on as a member of the college staff when something occurred that abruptly ended her horticultural career and threw her into a practical involvement with abnormal psychology.

This was the experience of coping with the effects of a nervous breakdown induced in her by a species of aggressive hypnosis – Svengali-like mesmerism might not be too strong a term – or what in later times has been described as brain washing. As a bright but no doubt uppity young student, she got the wrong side of the college warden, a formidable woman by all accounts, whose previous posts included being on the staff of the harem of the Emir of Afghanistan, and who ruled the place with a rod of iron. In some dispute over fund raising activities, the older woman, determined to make her rebellious student conform to her own version of events, subjected her to persistent and repetitious hectoring over a period of some hours, which left her in a state of nervous exhaustion that lasted for some weeks.

Well it did not break her spirit, and she crawled out of the abyss by stilling her racing mind by doing lots of simple calculations out of elementary arithmetic books, and in the longer term the traumatic experience led her towards the study of psychology. In the years just prior to the 1st World War, psychoanalytical theories were becoming the subject of considerable popular interest and the relatively infant science of psychology began to be taken more seriously. She no doubt felt it a great opportunity when she was offered a place in an experimental project known as the Medico-Psychological Clinic, in Brunswick Square, London.

Founded in 1914 by some progressive members of the medical profession, this organisation sought to treat functional nervous diseases and associated disorders by psychological as well as medical means. Realising that they also needed to educate their patients in the assumptions of elementary psychology and to instil the principles of basic mental hygiene, they enrolled a number of student/practitioners on a three year course. This largely consisted of on-the-job training, working under medical guidance to engage in what would nowadays probably be called therapeutic counselling.

The twenty-four-year-old Violet Firth seems to have been a very promising student counsellor, and before long was giving public lectures on the subject. These were later published in book form as *The Machinery of the Mind*, and honoured with a foreword by an eminent psychologist, A.G. Tansley, a Fellow of the Royal Society and author of a standard textbook on psychology.

Nonetheless, after a couple of years the bright student was beginning to become somewhat disillusioned with what she perceived as a general lack of success in the treatment of the patients. This came to a head in a particularly dramatic way with a strange case that included paranormal phenomena and some kind of obsessive behaviour that bordered on the criminal. It baffled everyone concerned but was resolved in a most unexpected manner by the intervention of a strange and remarkable man, Dr Theodore Moriarty. (There is no known connection I should say with the famous fictional detective of 221b Baker Street!)

An Irishman by birth, Moriarty had lived in South Africa for many years, a surveyor by profession, but with a keen interest in the anthropology of indigenous tribes. A keen Freemason, he had co-authored a couple of books on the subject, and also developed his own brand of esoteric philosophy that he called Universal Theosophy. So called, I imagine, through being derived from some of Madame Blavatsky's ideas but extended beyond her predominantly eastern emphasis.

Nor was he limited to philosophical speculation on the subject because, like Madame Blavatsky, he seems to have been skilled

Dr Theodore Moriarty

in some rather unusual psychic abilities. Some of these he appeared to use in finding a solution to this difficult case, effecting what to all intents and purposes seems to have been the exorcism on an obsessive and unquiet spirit that had been picked up somewhere on the killing fields of the Western Front.

Whatever the merits of the case, meeting Moriarty and seeing his methods in action had a profound effect upon Violet Firth. It was her first encounter with the esoteric side of things, and she saw whole new vistas of psychology opening up before her, completely unexplainable by conventional approaches to the subject. Indeed, such was the force of this revelation that she felt she could no longer, in good faith, continue working at the Clinic. There was a war on at the time, and volunteers were being sought to work on the land, so she responded to the patriotic call and joined the newly formed Women's Land Army.

She found herself, however, not tilling the land but working at an experimental laboratory researching alternative forms of diet – an urgent necessity as the country was threatened by food shortages through the German submarine blockade. In this she had some personal success, developing a form of protein out of soya, which became the topic of another of her early books, under the title of *The Soya Bean*, and her family spent some effort in encouraging its commercial development.

However, she had also begun to read all she could find in esoteric literature, and although she did not accept unequivocally all that she read, Annie Besant's popular classic *The Ancient Wisdom* not only impressed her but induced a powerful visionary experience, apparently in the high Himalayas, that caused her to feel she was being called to some kind of higher service. She also found herself becoming psychically sensitive in various ways, which may well have been the result of her continuing to study with Moriarty, who ran a variety of courses for personal students on various esoterically related subjects. This included his own brand of co-masonry, in which ceremonial activities she was a founding member, in 1919.

Evidently not content with confining all her eggs to one basket, in this same year she also enrolled in the Alpha et Omega Temple of what is still called the Hermetic Order of the Golden Dawn, although this famous esoteric fraternity had long since changed its name. The lodge of which she became a member was headed by the novelist J.W. Brodie-Innes and by Moina MacGregor Mathers, widow of the one of the principle founders of the Golden Dawn. All members of this organisation took on an aspirational motto, and the one she chose was *Deo Non Fortuna* – God not Chance – which was to provide her with the pen name of Dion Fortune by which she is now universally known.

Her association with Moriarty ended with his death in 1923 but so impressed had she been with this charismatic teacher that she built a fictional character around him in a series of short stories for a popular magazine. She was convinced that conventional psychology was ignoring a whole range of human experience, and used these stories as means of drawing public attention to what she liked to call the "lesser known powers of the human mind". The first story, entitled *Blood Lust*, was a fictionalised account of the case that had so strongly impressed her when she first met Moriarty. The rest of the stories, which were published in volume form as *The Secrets of Dr. Taverner*, were for the most part adventures woven around commonly accepted esoteric theories, such as reincarnation, astral projection, and various possibilities of the abuses of mind power. Her concern with the pathologies of the subject was a logical extension to the unfortunate experiences that had led her into these studies in the first place, and before getting all this out of her system she went on to write a macabre blood and thunder occult novel, *The Demon Lover*, and a highly coloured account of some of her early experiences under the title *Psychic Self Defence*.

In emulation of what she had seen of the real life Moriarty she tried to develop similar powers. This included a technique that, while it might seem by its results to have been a form of trance mediumship, she insisted was not what is usually understood by the term trance. That she did not make her mind a blank, nor was her will in abeyance, but by means of intense concentration, the result of some years of hard practice, she shut out the sensations of the five physical senses, stilling her mind and concentrating upon the image of a desired communicator. Ideas then arose in the form of words, which were recorded by the friends who assisted her.

Experiments of this kind were being pursued on a broad front in these post-war years. The experience of four years of mechanised slaughter gave rise to a considerable interest in spiritualism on the part of the recently bereaved, and also challenged some of the assumptions as to what society was all about and where civilisation was going. There was thus an eagerness to seek the avenues to some kind of higher wisdom by whatever means.

Thus we see at much the same time the beginnings of the work of Alice Bailey in the role of an amanuensis of one of Madame Blavatsky's former mahatmas, resulting in a vast body of work including *A Treatise on Cosmic Fire*, *A Treatise on White Magic* and the five volumes of *A Treatise on the Seven Rays*. Coming out of the more western Golden Dawn tradition was a complex cosmology through the automatic writing of W.B. Yeats' wife Georgie, which he later published as *A Vision*, and which, whatever its metaphysical merits, inspired much of his subsequent poetry. Dion Fortune working in similar vein produced a body of work known as *The Cosmic Doctrine*, the abstruse and challenging contents of which are described as designed "to train the mind rather than to inform it." This rubric may be said to apply to much of this kind of material, which transcends the categories of the usual run of intellectual analysis by the lower mind in order to develop the intuitional faculties.

There then remains the identification of the originators of this kind of communication, which takes us back to what I called the equivalent of the Graal questions that I asked a little earlier. Where are they coming from? Who put them there? On what authority?

Dion Fortune had four principle identities through which she sought various levels and types of verbal instruction, and in my biography *Dion Fortune and the Inner Light* I have quoted extensively from surviving records, taking them at face value, along with the interpretation that she and her close colleagues put upon them, leaving readers to make their own assessment.

Dion Fortune was always ready to concede that they might well have their origin in her own subconscious, but nonetheless to obtain any worthwhile results in the first place, one has to take the images of the communicators at face value. Scepticism on this point can immediately block the flow.

This does not mean of course that blind credulity is the key to success. Nor that critical analysis should not come afterward in an assessment of the quality of the results obtained, which must stand or fall by their own merits.

Although if we are going to ask searching questions about this kind of thing, it behoves us to try to ask the right questions. And in my experience, debate over the validity of the supposed identity of such communicators is a great red herring. As one of them stated fairly early on, "what we are you cannot realise and it is a waste of time to try to do so but you can imagine us…and we can contact you through your imagination, and although your mental picture is not real or actual, the results of it are real and actual."

Nonetheless a great deal of time is spent in fruitless speculation along these lines. What these characters indubitably are, be they fact, fiction or somewhere in between, are tuning devices in the imagination, imaginal hooks for the atunement of consciousness.

When all was said and done, Dion Fortune was quite prepared to advise those who found their credulity strained about some of her necessary assumptions, to regard it all simply as an interesting psychological experiment, with any results adjudged upon their merits.

For my own part I have to say that what I have seen of Dion Fortune's work I regard as generally impressive, which is not to say that it does not vary in quality, as does all work of this nature, particularly when personal interests or emotions are concerned. Furthermore the quality and nature of such work is often determined by the assumptions and expectations of the people sitting with her. It is notable for example that when in contact with a source retailing medical information it all flowed more easily and significantly in the presence of her husband, who was a medical doctor. And at a period when he was no longer available, there is a marked difference in quality when working in the presence of a qualified doctor who had a sympathetic approach to what was going on, than in the presence of a sceptical one who was trying to put test questions all the time – which in the end proved abortive for everyone concerned.

As far as Dion Fortune was concerned when she put her faith in such contacts, whether or not they were the historical personalities they were assumed to be, things worked. How well they worked may perhaps be judged in the success or failure of the esoteric school which, at their instigation, she founded. For what is particularly striking about Dion Fortune's contacts is that they also had organisational aspirations.

This is never more evident than in an interchange that took place in late 1927 between one of them, an alleged former army officer killed at Ypres, David Carstairs, and Dion Fortune's husband, Dr. Thomas Penry Evans:

Carstairs: "Now do you see what these chaps are driving at?"
Dr Evans: "To establish a school on the basis of discipline."
Carstairs: "And they don't want molly-coddles. If you can't stand a hammering, go home, see? It is not a bit of use pretending it is a bed of roses; it isn't. There is a great deal of difference between half-ideals and true ideals. But we are not out for those short cuts to comfort. We are out for something much bigger than that. You can't say where it begins or ends."

And wherever it may be going to end, for the moment all we can say is that it still goes on, for here we are today.

They insisted throughout that they were neither omniscient nor omnipotent, but working under their guidance, together with a few happy coincidences, Dion Fortune found herself in possession of a sanctuary at the foot of Glastonbury Tor, and a large house in the west end of London in which to establish a headquarters.

With the growth and development of the organisation came a growth and development in the realisations, work and aims of Dion Fortune herself, as the propagandist of the 1920s gave place to the mature teacher of the 1930s. The new decade was heralded by publication of *The Esoteric Orders and their Work* and *The Training and Work of an Initiate* as she came to terms with the task of training up a responsible body of associates.

Then came the major work for which she is justly famous, her textbook *The Mystical Qabalah*. Written in monthly instalments for her house magazine between 1930 and 1934, it was published in 1935 and remains an acknowledged classic – not necessarily through its scholarship or orthodoxy, but through its approachability and clarity. The purpose behind its writing might well be summed up in Dion Fortune's definition of an occult fraternity: an association of people who are trained in a particular symbol system. An initiate may therefore be regarded as a dedicated person who has been trained in such a symbol system and who therefore possesses a key to traditional wisdom. The Tree of Life of the Qabalah being one such key and one such system.

But she did not stop at the idea of producing a lucid textbook for students, and went on to seek new ways of bringing this particular avenue of traditional wisdom before a wider public. Her first attempt at this was to commence a series of novels, *The Winged Bull*, *The Goat-Foot God* and *The Sea Priestess* in which she sought to demonstrate practical applications of some of the forces represented by the Spheres upon the central pillar of the Tree of Life.

The novels are creatures of their time to the extent that she tries to explore some of the relationships between the sexes in the conventional moral climate of the 1930s, but at another level they are thought-provoking instruction manuals of various forms of esoteric practice, the depth and subtlety of which has recently surprised me in currently preparing a book about them for the press.

At about this time she also made an important new contact (outer plane not inner plane!) in the person of the London University academic Bernard Bromage. He had been commissioned, somewhat to his surprise – or perhaps amazement might not be too strong a word – to give a series of Extension Lectures on *The Literature of the Occult*. Somewhat curious as to what kind of students he might find attending such a series he was intrigued to find Dion Fortune among them, whose *The Mystical Qabalah* and *The Goat-Foot God* he had recently read. Although homework was essentially a voluntary activity in extension lectures she willingly turned in essays which he found well written and thought-provoking, and he came to regard her as his star student. He was even more impressed after accepting her invitation to attend the performance of a Rite of Isis that she was currently staging at an old converted church that she had leased in Belgravia.

This was a somewhat novel attempt to draw public attention to mythopoeic themes by their dramatic representation, although not without precedent, for McGregor Mathers and his wife Moina had attempted much the same thing with some success in 1898 at the Théatre Bodiniere on the Rue Saint-Lazare in Paris. Dion Fortune's revival of the tradition no doubt figured in her mind as a logical extension to her recent fiction, for part of the script of the Rite is to be found in *The Sea Priestess* as well as in her then unfinished posthumously published novel *Moon Magic*.

I fancy that she may have also had at the back of her mind a powerfully moving experience at Glastonbury in 1920, when she attended an early performance of Rutland Boughton's faery music drama *The Immortal Hour*, with lyrics by Fiona Macleod, which had transferred to the London stage with considerable success.

At all events Bernard Bromage came away from one of these performances of the Rite of Isis much impressed, later stating it to be "one of the best attempts I have ever witnessed to stimulate the subconscious by means of 'pantomime' drawn from the more ancient records of the hierophant's art." I assume him to be using the term "pantomime" in a more restricted and technical sense than might be applied to a modern commercial example of that ancient art. At any rate, a close collaboration developed between the two of them and in the Autumn of 1937 they organised a series of lecture/discussion evenings devoted to the esoteric in literature, to which luminaries of the time were invited to speak, including Christina Foyle, Marjorie Bowen, Berta Ruck, Claude Houghton and Elliott

O'Donnell, and which reportedly attracted a large and intelligent audience.

At the same time Bromage put at Dion Fortune's disposal much of the material he had collected on Eastern religions including his translation of Hindu texts on tantrik yoga. This supplemented her own recent studies, which had been profoundly influenced by her discovery of Jane Harrison's *Prolegomena to the Study of Greek Religion*. Published as long ago as 1903 this ground breaking text was based upon ancient Greek ritual practices long before the Olympian gods gained their ascendancy, in an era of matriarchal religion when local earth goddesses were the power behind local heroes, and led in turn to a deep investigation of the cult of Dionysos with his wild rout of meneads and satyrs, and of Orpheus, the magical musician who could tame all things including the forces of the underworld.

Dionysian and Orphic revelries, tantrik yoga, Rites of Isis, to say nothing of the evocation of theories of animal magnetism in the polar interchange between the sexes as described in some of her novels, seem upon the face of it to be pretty hot stuff, and likely to cause one or two raised eyebrows. It may even be responsible for an entry in a recent academic guide to esoteric societies that lists the Society of the Inner Light as being largely devoted to sex magic. All I can say is that if that is the best that the combined resources of the Sorbonne and the University of New York can come up with, then I think their performance currently falls somewhat short of their reputation. Although I concede their difficulty in attempting to sum up a decade's endeavour in the space of half a dozen words.

Let it be said that Dion Fortune was dedicated to ends and means rather above the self indulgences and self deceptions of what commonly passes for sex magic. She wrote up her conclusions in a series of articles under the title *The Circuit of Force* in her magazine between February 1939 and August 1940, in which her general theme is the recovery and practical application of what she called "the lost secrets of the West".

Some of her perceptions have since been broadly recognised. The key ideas she derived from Greek Mystery Rites included the

Dr Thomas Penry Evans and Dion Fortune

image of Persephone as a goddess within the Earth with whom mankind needs to be in a creative respectful relationship. The idea of a goddess whose realm is within the Earth has been gaining currency in modern times even if not always couched in such terms. She is sometimes referred to as Gaea, deriving from the very ancient earth goddess who in Jane Harrison's book, as in Dion Fortune's Rite of Isis, was known as Ge.

In its wider aspects this embraces the whole field of ecological responsibility for the environment and for the non-human species that inhabit the Earth along with ourselves.

The ancient goddess appeared at many locations to inspire the local hero and to represent the sovereignty of the land. This local element is not a matter of petty provincialism but a recognition of the uniqueness of specific tracts of land, in relation to the natural flora and fauna, geophysical construction and human beings living upon it. Whoever lives off this tract of land becomes its subject and whoever seeks to tend and defend it becomes wedded to its sovereignty. This is a concept that might bear with deeper consideration in the face of current globalisation and some of the evils it brings with it.

Dionysos, as the 'twice born' discoverer of the vine and of divine inebriation, is an expression of the inner forces and divine potential of the human individual. That is to say the forces of the underworld when denied expression can lead to catastrophe. A dramatic example of this is to be found in Euripides' play *The Bacchae* which has relevance to both personal psychology and to spirituality, with the god Dionysos as the vital stream of spiritual energy, the totality of man's forces, to whose service the meneads must be dedicated. Dion Fortune, in the pre-war period, looked at this in terms of the repressive moral attitudes of her day, which were assumed to be the necessary price for maintaining a stable society. We might today ask whether repression of certain unconscious dynamics has ever been a problem in the attitudes of the West to the East – and not least the Middle East. Or indeed the Third World as a whole.

But passing to a more technical side of the subject, Dion Fortune set about comparing the Qabalistic system of the west with the eastern systems of Yoga. Her reasons for doing so being the practical use of the psychic centres, at their various levels. This takes us into the realms of what is commonly called the etheric double and concepts, such as animal magnetism, that have long been discarded by scientific thought.

In recently preparing an edition of *The Circuit of Force* for book publication, together with a commentary to fill in some of the speculative blanks she left, I discovered that there was a great deal of 19th century work along these lines that seemed to have been thrown into the discard more through changing scientific fashion and clinical expediency than hard evidence. Be that as it may, Dion Fortune was engaged in medical aspects of this kind of work from 1927 with her husband, Dr Thomas Penry Evans, in what could have developed into a real life version of Dr Taverner and his esoteric clinic. Later she worked with whatever sympathetic doctors she could find – much of it clinical and diagnostic work that has recently surfaced to be published as *Principles of Esoteric Healing*.

However, all the promising developments of the 1930s came to an abrupt halt with the declaration of war in September 1939, which put a stop to most group and publishing activities.

Undeterred, Dion Fortune kept in touch with her students and associates by means of a one page weekly letter, which became the vehicle for a far flung meditation group. Whether or not the group played any influential role in the state of the group soul of the nation, the letters are a unique record of performing occult work under difficulties. Dion Fortune may perhaps be unique in the annals of esoteric teaching in giving instruction on how best to meditate whilst under aerial bombardment.

Ten years ago, when an edited version of these letters was published, she was criticised for what a younger generation felt to be her dated patriotism. It is therefore interesting, and I must say personally moving, since the events of September 11th 2001, to find some citizens of New York writing in appreciation of what she had to say about holding to one's values and inner serenity when under physical threat, to the extent that a new American edition has been called for.

The war years also saw Dion Fortune's deeper interest and involvement in the Arthurian legend. This began, as does much of lasting significance in the esoteric world, not with any conscious intellectual decision, but in response to spontaneous images that began to arise in her meditation group at this time. Of King Arthur, of Merlin, as well as the Blessed Virgin and the Christ, that built up over a period of weeks as a kind of pyramidal mandala. However, it did not end there, for she embarked on a period of intensive work that resulted in a script known as *The Arthurian Formula*.

Students of literature have often remarked upon the hold that the legends of Arthur have exercised on the imagination of western man. One theory favoured by Dion Fortune was that they enshrine a secret Mystery Tradition that stems from immense antiquity, a star lore inherited by the Celtic invaders from their Bronze Age and even Neolithic predecessors, and preserved in their myth and legend.

Taken to its ultimate extension of each conquering race taking over the ancient beliefs of its predecessors, she was quite ready to enter the realms of what many might see as the bizarre, with evocations of Atlantis as part of proto-Arthurian dynamics. Indeed a respected academic, whilst acknowledging Dion Fortune's importance in certain areas of popular culture, takes this simply to be evidence of scientific ignorance and lack of education on her part.

However, at risk of being tarred by the same academic brush, I think such assumptions may be a little too glib, for the Atlantean continent looms too large in the mists of the collective imagination to be too readily dismissed. Like God, even if it did not exist it might be necessary to invent it. Certainly, at the most superficial level, the legend of a whole civilisation plunging to destruction as a result of its own overweening pride, corruption and technical folly is something we might do well to take to heart in our current situation of technological and political hubris.

That serves well as a simple parable, but may there not be a deeper level than that? As with what we have said about the identity of inner communicators, it is important that we ask the right questions. If some source of power or influence does not exist at one level of perception, might it not nonetheless exist very markedly at another? In which case, the willing suspension of disbelief in such a mythopoeic paradigm or helpful fiction might serve to tune consciousness to some source of wisdom accessible only to different modes of perception.

Let us think for a moment in terms of Tolkien's vast imagination. Good conservative Roman Catholic though he was, when he set out to reinvent a mythology for the north west, he found himself taking on board the whole panoply of Atlantis, albeit under the name of Númenor. And if we take a look at *The Silmarillion*, of which the massive and celebrated *The Lord of the Rings* forms but a very minor part, we can find ourselves being invited to enter a different perception of historical reality altogether.

A great source of power and wisdom to the west has been celebrated in many ancient tales, including that of Perseus, that has been projected into the circumpolar stars. Could it be that the west of the Hesperides, of Atalanta, and the like, might be accessed not by travelling in a terrestrial westerly direction, which simply takes us round the globe until we end up where we started, but by going out directly in a straight line, so to speak, beyond the ambit and the orbit of the physical Earth. What kind of imaginal territory do we enter then?

Rudolf Steiner, an individual of no small education, who took seriously and edited the scientific works of Göethe, was not afraid to take this Atlantean business head on. And in his view of things, what is being talked about in this tradition is a metaphysical history of consciousness, not simply of the physical vehicles that we inhabit in our brief sojourn on this terrestrial coil. Do very ancient memories, of other times and other climes in a cosmic sense, provoke us to seek for that which is hardly to be found in terms of three dimensional space and time?

But to return to the more parochial safety of King Arthur, the Knights of the Table Round, of Merlin, the Ladies of the Lake, and the Grail as more conventionally understood. We know little of the historical Arthur, the Romano-British Count of the Saxon shore evoked by historians. But in the study of myth and legend, history is not important; its bearing is only indirect. We are concerned with the poetic imagination rather than prosaic fact.

The mechanism is very important. Powerful archetypes of racial consciousness, or wisdom from ancestral sources if you like, make their appearance by crystallising about the deeds of men or women of vision. The vision, however inadequately it might have been expressed in the historical event, is celebrated by the poets, bards, or romancers, whoever has the antennae of inspiration and the ability to tell a story that will interest and inspire their hearers.

Arthurian legend is unique, as it has come down to us today via the 12th and 13th century romancers, in that it provides a complete run through from the depths of our primeval spiritual yearnings to the heights of mystical experience. From the ancient traditions of the cauldron of inspiration and rebirth won from the King of the Underworld to Galahad the perfect Christian knight returning his soul to God after achieving the Grail Quest, the visions complement each other and give a complete picture of the way of achievement in the evolution of human consciousness.

As a great synthesiser, Dion Fortune was able to bring much of this material within bounds and largely through her lucid grasp of the Qabalistic Tree of Life. For in this system it is not necessary to be confined to the perceptions of the Qabalistic rabbis. Part of the genius of whoever formulated the system was that it genuinely does have a universal application. It provides what has been well described as a map of the soul of man and of the universe – under the assumption that the microcosm which is man is a reflection of the macrocosm which is the objective world, at all its levels, in which we live. This means that as well as there being a physical equivalent to our physical bodies, in the physical world about us, there are subtler objective equivalents to the subtler psychological levels that also form our being.

Nor is this limited to the four-fold structure of the personality, which in the Jungian structure, which Dion Fortune favoured, equates to the four lower spheres of the Tree of Life. There exist higher spheres on the Tree of Life just as there are higher levels of

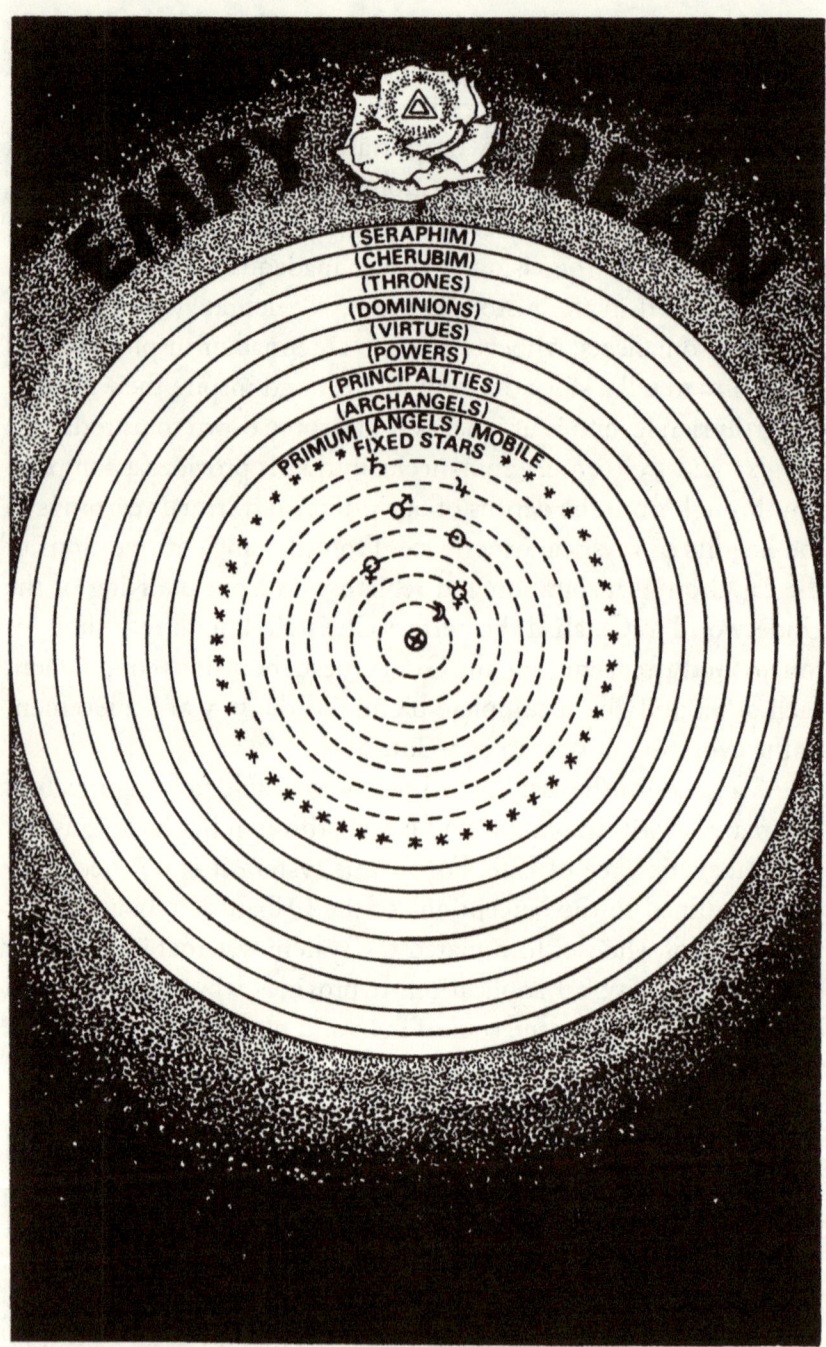

The structure of the Heavenly Spheres as described by Dante

consciousness within ourselves. By tracing out and treading in the imagination some of these paths we may be led to an experience of the opening up of our own higher consciousness, which is by no means an entirely subjective experience, for it brings with it an awareness, through higher doors of perception, of an objective world of souls or spiritual world.

Some of these paths and these worlds have been delineated, in a less structured manner, in many of the myths and legends that have inspired the human race. One that I discovered to be a potent one was the first occasion that I attempted a little practical work at a public workshop, some twenty-five years ago. Not wishing to load my listeners with too much in the way of Qabalistic symbolism I took a more familiar system, that lies very close to the structure of the Tree of Life, the masterpiece of western literature, Dante's *Paradiso*.

From an imagined vision of the Earthly Paradise at the antipodes of earthly life as we currently know it, we rose in imagination through the heavens described by Dante, which concur exactly with the spheres of the Tree of Life. From the ideal state of Earth through the heavens of the Moon, Mercury, Venus, the Sun, Mars, Jupiter, Saturn to the Fixed Stars and angelic sphere of the Primum Mobile, through to the Rosa Mystica riding high in the Empyrean of Eternity. And then slowly descending in the midst of a slow snow fall of white and golden petals from the mystic rose back to whence we had started.

This medieval vision may not have sat very close to the scientific mapping of the solar system in a post-Copernican age, but nonetheless those who travelled this ancient way seemed to know very well that they had journeyed somewhere to some purpose. To their surprise it brought tears of joy and wonder to a number who for the first time, and by such simple means, had learned at first hand something of being exposed to what Dante described as "the Love that moves the earth and all the stars."

And it taught a salutary lesson to me. That here in a source readily available from any decent book store, was a practical means toward mystical and esoteric experience. For the study of Dante tends to be obfuscated by footnotes on his allusions to various political and other events and personalities of his time. Another instance, I suggest, of having the vision before us, but not asking the right questions about what we see.

And to be fair, for we can blind ourselves with esoteric knowledge too, no great need to have made a detailed study of Qabalah, or the oriental chakras, or sought study in an esoteric school for the technique of 'rising on the planes'. All you have to do is believe in it, and then do it.

Thus I suppose the reason behind the alchemical adage that the philosopher's stone is about us everywhere, but our eyes are just too dim to see it. With the eyes of the imagination however, and the desire to tread the path rather than to talk learnedly about it, we might find and pick up a few pearls more easily.

We have, as that wise and simple man William Blake enjoined us, simply to cleanse the doors of perception, and beyond that, to ask the right questions of what, as a result, we may observe. Thus our quest might best be defined, not to rediscover the lost secrets of the west, but simply to stumble upon the glaringly obvious ones we were too clever by half to see!

THE WESTERN ESOTERIC TRADITION AND POPULAR CULTURE

Talk given by Gareth Knight at the Temenos Academy, 10th December 2003

ON THE face of it the Western Esoteric Tradition and Popular Culture may seem a contradiction in terms. After all, 'esoteric' means 'for the few', whilst 'popular culture' is obviously for the many. So how are these two reconciled? Where do they meet?

I have to say, in a manner that is often clandestine and generally misunderstood. And this is not helped by the fact that the Esoteric Tradition, because it is an embodiment of the Perennial Philosophy, has an element of permanence about it, whilst popular culture is essentially transitory and ephemeral, a thing of the moment, ever changing. So how does the permanent and the esoteric shine through the temporal and popular?

An example that comes to mind lies in the Tarot cards, which have an interesting role in cultural history since their appearance five hundred years ago in Renaissance Italy. The first book I ever wrote, a somewhat esoteric tome, attempted an analysis of their relationship to the Tree of Life of the Qabalah. The cards were certainly more esoteric than popular then, at any rate in London in 1961. I had the utmost difficulty in finding a set of Tarot cards on sale in the whole of Britain, and where found, they were likely to be highly priced antiquarian rarities.

Dion Fortune and the Lost Secrets of the West

But in the early nineteen seventies some kind of cultural explosion occurred that shot them into popularity, albeit as a means of fortune telling. They have even been featured in a James Bond film, in a special design no doubt crafted in the mystic shrines of Hollywood. Anyhow the fact remains that nowadays there is a plethora of Tarot packs to choose from, a hundred and fifty at the very least. Nor do we have to make an esoteric pilgrimage to Watkins or the Atlantis Bookshop, for they can also be found on display as novelty items in various shops and department stores. Perhaps not quite so much now as in recent years, for as I said, popular culture is ephemeral.

Popular culture is also regional and over the several hundred years since its first appearance the Tarot had certainly been popular in Italy, Switzerland and southern France, not in any esoteric capacity, but as a popular card game. Any relevance to the Western Esoteric Tradition was not proclaimed until the end of the eighteenth century. Then, after an efflorescence of popular fortune telling in post-revolutionary France, they were declared an integral part of Qabalistic symbolism by the occultist Eliphas Lévi in the 1860s, and have been so regarded in certain esoteric circles to this day.

It had always been my assumption that elements of esoteric philosophy were deliberately built into the Tarot from the start. That, possibly along with some of the paintings of Botticelli, they had been commissioned as a set of meditation symbols, as a result of an interest in the Hermetic texts recently translated by Marsilio Ficino. This assumption has recently been challenged by a redoubtable academic team led by Michael Dummett, former Wykeham Professor of Logic at the University of Oxford. Their contention is that they are not, and have never been, anything other than playing cards, around which occultists have weaved their own private fantasies.

Their works on the subject, Michael Dummett's own *The Game of Tarot* in 1980, followed more recently by *A Wicked Pack of Cards – the Origins of the Occult Tarot* and *A History of the Occult Tarot 1870-1970* are, I have to say, models of dedicated scholarly research which the esoteric field sorely needs. But although I can lay no very great claims to academic distinction, particularly in the field of art history, I do reckon to recognise esoteric significance when I see it.

Michael Dummett, with whom I developed a quite cordial relationship in the course of his later research, was rather surprised that I should be quite relaxed over claims of his which had set other esoteric aficionados buzzing round his ears like a nest of hornets. And I suppose it is understandable for esoteric students, at a stage of development when implicit belief is important to them, to tend to view academic research with the same fear and suspicion as religious fundamentalists regard textual criticism of the Bible. However, my own position remains that we have nothing to fear from the facts. It is the way the facts are interpreted that is important.

So whether the Tarot Trumps were consciously designed by a school of Hermetic philosophers, or whether some inspired artisan simply plucked images out of the air, or out of his own head, or pinched them from a common stock of Justice, Victory, Sun, Moon and the like, makes very little difference to me in pragmatic terms. Whatever its historical provenance, in the Tarot we have a collection of evocative images that are capable of esoteric interpretation.

I know this from my own experience in training myself and others over a number of years. If we chose to put this in terms of psychology, we might say that the origin of the symbols lies in the collective unconscious, along with a great bank of other mythopoeic images, of which the Tarot Trumps may be a random but nonetheless very useful selection.

Nor does it matter very much that different occultists should have different interpretations of their significance. For we are not operating according to the laws of logic. A symbol *is* what a symbol *does*. It may act in a different way from one individual to another, from one group of individuals to another, in different locations of space or different periods of time. Trying to make sense of all this is a matter of balancing intellect and intuition, for neither are really adequate on their own.

Now the popular mind will make a fortune telling system out of anything. There once was the system of Virgilian lots, opening the pages of the poems of Virgil at random in order to obtain an oracular message. And I have also seen the method used in pious hands with regard to the Bible.

Perhaps more striking nowadays, even than the Tarot, is the utilisation in popular journalism of the signs of the zodiac, for daily, weekly or monthly star readings based upon the month of one's birth. This is all part of the entertainment industry and a far cry from the extremely complex and ancient art of the astrologers. I do not claim to be one of this dedicated band, as I manage to muddle through my life fairly well on a combination of mother wit, luck and intuition, with a little help from my wife and my friends. Although I have to say that I am prepared to concede that there may be more to this ancient art than meets the vulgar or the academic eye. Not only because I have come across one or two remarkable astronomical coincidences, but also because something that is ever on the periphery of human popular consciousness must have something in it somewhere.

But we need not remain dabbling in the shallows of popular fortune telling, for some of the deeper issues of the influence of the Western Esoteric Tradition on Popular Culture are to be found in popular literature. Here again I hope that the terms 'popular' and 'literature' are not regarded by anyone as a contradiction in terms. If so I ask you to bear with me and to include popular versifying in the realm of the poetic, and genre fiction in the realm of literature, as broadly understood.

The first person who comes to mind in this respect is the poet Alfred Noyes. He is somewhat neglected nowadays, but in terms of the number of his books sold he was probably the most successful poet of the 20th century. His narrative verse attracted a huge following in the English speaking world, and although he flunked his degree at Oxford in 1902, because he was having a meeting with his publisher on a crucial day of his finals, he was later awarded the honorary degree of Doctor of Literature at Yale in 1913 and appointed visiting Professor of English Literature at Princeton from 1914 to 1923. In light of his current neglect it may perhaps be useful if I quote the opening lines of one of his successful narrative poems:

> The wind was a torrent of darkness among the gusty trees,
> The moon was a ghostly galleon tossed upon cloudy seas,
> The road was a ribbon of moonlight over the purple moor,
> And the highwayman came riding –
> > Riding – riding –
> *The highwayman came riding, up to the old inn door.*

This is good old rumpty-tumpty stuff, and with a good romantic story line of how Bess the inn-keeper's daughter went to her death to save her highwayman lover from the red coat troopers waiting to arrest him. It might not be great poetry, but my goodness it was popular, and it is one of the most anthologised narrative poems in the English language.

But we may search for his name in vain in any modern reference book of English literature. The most recent academic comment upon his work I have found is by Professor David Perkins in the Harvard University Press *History of Modern Poetry* of 1976. And I quote:

> Like most poets of his day, he celebrated English landscape, history, and character, which he conceived only in literary conventions. He has an elvish England of twilight witchery, turnstyles, and cottages; a merry England of country roads and inns, highwaymen and red coats. *Drake*, his blank-verse epic in twelve books, follows the adventures of the seagoing hero up to the Armada, and sees in Drake and in England embodiments of political and spiritual freedom. His patriotism is almost embarrassingly simpleminded and fervent, as may be seen also in his *Tales of the Mermaid Tavern*, which deals with the same period of history.

Now my interest in Alfred Noyes derives precisely from his choice of subject matter, which runs closely in parallel with esoteric tradition insofar as it has to do with the world of heroes. With

Noyes this was first apparent in his long epic poem on Sir Francis Drake. Now you may wonder what this may have to do with the esoteric tradition. And the answer lies in the interface between history and legend.

Some historical figures develop a certain charisma that manifests in their becoming the focus of a body of legend. Drake, in his pioneering voyage round the world, is one such figure. The theme of a long voyage to distant and unknown lands can be a form of initiatory experience, as it is a paradigm of the processes of the human soul, going right back to ancient Greece and the adventures of Odysseus or the Voyage of the Argo. In addition, Drake was one of the first 'planetary' men. Someone who had actually gone round this globe in space that we inhabit, as significant to the progress and self awareness of the human race as are spacemen in our own age.

It is therefore not surprising that over the years a certain body of legend grew up about him, ranging from his galloping over Dartmoor to cause springs to rise up to provide a water supply for Plymouth, to a cannonball falling from heaven to prevent his girlfriend Elizabeth Sydenham from marrying another while he was away on his world voyage. The cannon ball can still be seen incidentally if you go to the lady's ancestral home. Spanish sailors called him El Draco, which associates him with the circumpolar stars of Draco – the world dragon – so that in another sense his fame is elevated to the stars, and to a constellation that has particular traditional roots with creativity both human and planetary. I know that to any rationally rooted person, and not least to Professors of Logic, or even of English Literature, this may sound like a concoction of high flown *non sequiturs*. Nonetheless, some of us whose expertise runs in other directions consider that there may be some kind of 'string theory' connecting them.

This also applies to Noyes' *Tales of the Mermaid Tavern*, which is an evocation of other charismatic figures of the Elizabethan age, including William Shakespeare, Christopher Marlowe, Ben Jonson, Mary Queen of Scots, Dick Wittington and Sir Walter Ralegh amongst others. And despite what Professor Perkins might have us believe, this is no mere sentimental nostalgia. To put it in psychological terms, these characters and others like them form the equivalent of archetypes in the racial or national unconscious. And if you begin surfing the net of inner space you are very soon likely to come up against them, and you do not have to be a paid up member of an esoteric organisation to realise this. The implications are all too clear, once we realise that images like this can act as a focus for emotive convictions to do with national or regional identities, and the heroism, the ideals or fanaticism that can sometimes go with them. Certainly they can be manipulated on behalf of political ideologies, from regional separatist movements in nation states, through to their wholesale abuse in totalitarian states or in racist movements. On the other hand they can be a clarion call to national identity in times of need, as was Sir Laurence Olivier's filmic evocation of Shakespeare's Henry V in the 2nd World War.

And these archetypal figures are not necessarily confined to a national level, which Professor Perkins seems to have overlooked. Noyes developed this in his later work, in a trilogy called *The Torch Bearers* in which he celebrated great discoverers in the whole range of human endeavour. First in the realm of discoverers of the stars, with Copernicus, Tycho Brahe, Kepler, Galileo, Newton, and William and John Herschel; then in more earth centred natural philosophers and scientists from Pythagoras and Aristotle, through Avicenna and Leonardo, to Linnaeus, Lamarck, Göethe and Darwin. Finally, he celebrated the miracles of modern technology represented by the invention of radio; that is, the utilisation of unseen waves and vibrations that have nowadays become not only scientifically respectable but generally taken for granted.

These figures are treated by Noyes in an evocative and highly imaginative way. A typical example is of Tycho Brahe who, on his island of Venusia, between Sweden and Denmark, built a great foursquare castle called the Uraniburg, devoted to the study of the stars. An Odin-like figure, a nobleman who wears a gold mask, he forms part of a fourfold magical mandala, with his peasant wife Christina, his assistant Johannes Kepler, and his faithful servant, the half witted but prophetically gifted Jeppe. All this is based upon history, but history being transformed into legend, which is a fashion of speaking deeply to concerns of the soul.

Now if this should seem like an abuse of history, I would tend to counter with the argument that so is most historical writing. Our view of the past is conditioned very much by what we are in the present, and so it is arguable if there is any such thing as truly objective history. This of course is no news to professional historians, who have learned to live with it, so I simply state how I am nailing my own colours to the mast. Which is close to Thomas Carlyle, the sage of Chelsea, who also wrote a book *On Heroes and Hero Worship*, recognising various forms of heroes as divinities, prophets, poets, priests, men of letters, or kings, and whose tumultuous treatment of the French Revolution remains a challenge to more prosaic treatments of the period in giving us a chance to experience and reconsider what it all meant. A treatment that John Stuart Mill called an epic poem as much as a history. And what is wrong, one might ask, with historians being asked to be epic poets?

But there is another level, that lies beyond the legendary, and that is the mythopoeic, which accounts for another strand in the work of Alfred Noyes. If we go back to that early poem of *The Highwayman* we find that not only was it the most popular thing he ever wrote but that its opening lines came to him in an unusual way.

He had just come down from Oxford and was living in a cottage on Bagshott Heath in Sussex, which in those days was still quite wild country. And the first lines of the poem floated into his mind from the sound of the wind in the trees. What is significant about this is that, although he was in many ways a very conventional kind of chap, Alfred Noyes confessed to an inner guide that came to him first in childhood in west Wales, when he spent many hours in the woods overlooking the sea near his home.

As he describes in his autobiography, *Two Worlds for Memory*, it was here he fed his imagination, not only on the natural sights and sounds amongst the bracken and the fir trees, but on the images within the books that he brought with him. These, remarkably for a nine-year-old boy, included Keats, Wordsworth and Walter Scott as well as Spenser's *Faerie Queen*. And although he understood little of the intellectual content of Spenser's poem, its bewitching imagery merged into the woods that grew around his boyhood den; which was a clearing no more than twelve feet square, on a cliff face overlooking the tops of the pine trees below, and with a clear view over the western sea. This he discovered to be a truly magical place, for beyond the intimations of beauty and design he found in the natural world about him, and the visions that were aroused by his reading, there came into his head the presence of another. A being not seen by anyone else, a strange fey creature who seemed to slip into his awareness like the dappled shadows of the leaves upon the page of an open book. And so the name he gave to this faery visitant was naturally 'Shadow-of-a-Leaf'.

There are, of course, many children who have imaginary companions, which fade with approaching adulthood as "the shades of the prison house begin to close", but in Alfred Noyes' case, Shadow-of-a-Leaf never left him, and he later described him as "an invisible friend…a kind of Ariel who could open doors into unseen worlds." Shadow-of-a-Leaf could not have been far away when Noyes wrote his first famous narrative poem and he also appears from time to time in his later work, either as character or as inspirer.

Noyes, who was naturally a bit defensive about this kind of thing, chose to call Shadow-of-a-Leaf no more than "a psychological curiosity", which I have to say is a device that I and some of my esoteric colleagues choose to fall back upon, on occasion, when challenged as to the validity of some of our experiences. However, there is in fact a wide gulf between psychology and the inner worlds of the esoteric tradition, despite the superficial parallels. Fundamentally psychology is subjective, a mental sphere whose circumference is bounded by the human skull. The esoteric world is objective, a cosmic sphere whose centre is to be found within each human spirit.

Alfred Noyes never went out of his way to pursue the esoteric or the psychic, and found his spiritual home in the Roman Catholic church, but he seems to have been a natural intuitive and mystic, for as he says in his autobiography, after someone had been vainly trying to interest him in spiritualism, "Let me add that for years I have felt quite certain that communications from the invisible world do come unpredictably, in quite a different way, subtle as the language of music or the colours of an evening sky, in aid and consolation to the lonely heart of man."

This accounts for an early strand in his work, the World of Faery, in two long dramatic poems and a play about Sherwood Forest based on the Robin Hood legends. They do not read too well nowadays, but appealed to Edwardian sentiment sufficiently for Beerbohm Tree to want to produce one of them as a follow up to Barrie's *Peter Pan*, whilst W.B. Yeats was keen to have another of Noyes' poems chanted to the accompaniment of a psaltery at an Abbey Theatre production. For a better exposition of this type of dynamic however, we can turn to a more recent and popular evoker of the mythopoeic in J.R.R. Tolkien.

Like Noyes, Tolkien was theologically quite happy to be a member of the Roman Catholic church, although he is also lauded by neo-pagans because of the dedication and purpose with which he set out to write and renovate the fragmented mythology of north-western Europe. This amounted almost to a sense of religious mission, because he firmly believed, not only in the power of the imagination, but in its sanctity.

Whether or not directly influenced by Coleridge's celebrated views on the matter, or Blake's, he was firmly convinced that imaginative writing was a species of sub-creation, particularly in the realm of myth-making and legend. Indeed that spiritual truths could be revealed by it. He expounds his views on this in his important essay *On Fairy Stories* where he coins the term Faerian Drama. This is an ability to produce fantasies within the minds of others "with a realism and immediacy beyond the compass of any human mechanism." This has the effect of transporting the individual into another world, and although it has sometimes been compared to dreaming, or even identified with it, it is a dream that some other mind is weaving.

This is quite startling stuff. He is not simply talking about his own mind affecting the reader's mind. He is talking about his own mind having tapped a certain level which the reader's can then tap through the reading of his words. The physical world is what he calls the primary world of reality, which is the same for elves or for men. It is a reality however that happens to be differently valued and perceived by the two races.

Preferring to avoid the word 'magic' because of its misleading and historically dubious associations, and not much enamoured of the psycho-philosophical term 'secondary belief', Tolkien prefers to use the word 'enchantment'.

Magic, in its vulgar sense, claims to produce changes in the primary world about us. Of such, it seems to me, are the highly popular but fundamentally shallow adventures of Harry Potter, which I see largely as good old-fashioned school stories with a liberal dash of wish fulfilment fantasy. Enchantment, on the other hand, evokes a secondary world in which two worlds, the faery and human, can meet.

Writing or telling fairy stories, in Tolkien's view, is the nearest human equivalent to this elven enchantment. Whether approached from the human or the elven side, enchantment is not a self-centred desire for power. Nor is it a vehicle for glamour, bewitchment or delusion. Rather is it a seeking for shared enrichment, with partners in co-operative and delightful enterprise.

There has of course been a long tradition of the mythopoeic in varying degrees in children's literature starting from the mid nineteenth century with the collectors of fairy stories such as the Brothers Grimm. These were translated into English in 1853, the same year as the works of Hans Christian Andersen, who happened to be a great teller of tales rather than just a collector of them. It is arguable whether such material is restricted in its appeal to any particular age group and although Andersen's first edition was entitled *Stories told to the Children* this was soon changed to *Stories for the Household*.

It was not long before the baton was picked up by the myth-making George MacDonald, with his *Phantastes*, and *Lilith*, hardly stories for the young, the first of which had a profound effect upon C.S. Lewis. Certainly Tolkien saw any association of children with fairy stories as no more than an accident of domestic history, and thought that children as a class neither like them more nor understand them better than adults do. And that fairy story, if it is worth anything at all, is worthy of being written for and read by adults.

And he means *read* by, not studied, far less analysed. Nor was he content with Coleridge's definition of a "suspension of disbelief" which he thought but a halfway house to complete imaginal involvement in the Secondary World of fantasy. Fantasy, in his view, was "not a lower but a higher form of Art, indeed the most nearly pure form, and so (when achieved) the most potent." And to present this Secondary World of fantasy so vividly as to command Secondary Belief, or beyond that of Enchantment, demands a special skill, what he called "a kind of elvish craft". As he went on to say: "Few attempt such difficult tasks. But when they are attempted and in any degree accomplished then we have a rare achievement of Art: indeed narrative art, story-making in its primary and most potent mode."

This comes very close to the aims of the practical worker in the esoteric realm. But in the literary field we have not only Tolkien's great sagas in *The Silmarillion* and its offshoots, plus *The Lord of the Rings* but also a few shorter pieces, such as *Smith of Wootton Major*, which in its way is every bit as instructive and important as his essay *On Fairy Stories*.

In the specific realm of fantasy in children's literature we have of course had a thriving tradition over the past hundred and fifty years. Beginning perhaps with the blind Irish story teller Frances Browne, and *Granny's Wonderful Chair* in which the little girl Snowflower can sit in the chair and say "Chair of my grandmother, tell me a story" or "Chair of my grandmother, take me on a journey," to be transported through time and space. The line continues after George MacDonald's *At the Back of the North Wind* and *The Princess and the Goblin* to Rudyard Kipling with *Puck of Pook's Hill* and *Rewards and Fairies* where the children evoke a sprite, a kind of *genius loci* who takes them on journeys through time that are rather more significant than history lessons for primary school children. And Kipling's mentor to some extent in this genre was Edith Nesbit, whose esoteric connections included membership of the Hermetic Order of the Golden Dawn, and who wrote a number of tales of children coming to terms with various otherworldly creatures to take them on magical journeys through time and space in *The Psammead,* or *Five Children and It,* in *The Phoenix and the Carpet* and *The Amulet* to name but three. John Masefield later tried his hand with *The Midnight Folk* and *The Box of Delights* and in the latter half of the twentieth century a whole galaxy of writers appeared, of whom Alan Garner demands particular mention for his close involvement with the esoteric traditions of his own neck of the woods, around Alderley Edge. His work also demonstrates a gradual transition from conventional juvenile fantasy in *The Weirdstone of Brisingamen* and *The Moon of Gomrath* through increasingly adult modes via *Elidor, The Owl Service* and *Red Shift* to a literary tour de force in *The Stone Book* quartet, where inner and outer worlds meet in symbolic and real juxtaposition through four generations of a local family.

However, it is popular culture rather than literary fiction that concerns us for the moment, which demands a consideration of the visual media of television and film and how they are likely to be an adequate vehicle for the esoteric tradition.

In this respect we can draw a salutary lesson from P.L. Travers, who in 1934 launched an ancient goddess in disguise upon the modern world. One who was blown in by the wind and blown away when the wind changed. Who understood the language of birds, defied gravity, carried all her belongings in a magical bag, could make medicine pleasant, heard what the wind said, and had control over stars. Amongst her often amoral and subversive enchantments, stars came to earth, marble statues ran naked in the park, babies chewed fingers snapped from hands of witches, innocent passers-by were whirled into the air. The name of the goddess was Mary Poppins.

She was, and is, a far cry from the sweet and glamorous confection of the Hollywood film of 1964, which goes to show that modern modes of mass entertainment may not always be best fitted to preserve ancient traditions. It is indeed, quite difficult nowadays to read the Mary Poppins books without the image of Julie Andrews singing *A Spoonful of Sugar makes the Medicine go down* rising up before one. Miss Travers hated the film and steadfastly refused to allow any sequel or musical stage adaptation.

Pamela Travers took the esoteric tradition very seriously. Although born in Australia, of Scottish and Irish parents, she made her way back to Ireland and became a close acquaintance of writers of the Irish Celtic renaissance. Of course going to Ireland did not necessarily mean discovering an implicit connection between esoteric and popular culture. As she soon found out, not all her Irish friends and relations shared her enthusiasm for friends like Yeats or George Russell and bluntly told her, "We don't like you gallivanting around with men who see fairies!"

Nor did she have much luck when she went searching for the Isle of Inisfree just before she first met Yeats. As she tells us in her essay *Only Connect*, she happened to be travelling to Dublin by train when she suddenly realised that it went past Lough Gill, which is where Yeats' poetic island of Innisfree is supposed to be. On impulse she determined to visit the island, and leaping from the train charged a boatman to take her there.

"Ach, ther's no such place," he said.

"Oh, but there is, I assure you. W.B. Yeats wrote about it."

"And who would he be?"

She told him.

"Ah, I know them, those poets, always stravaiging through their minds, inventing outlandish things. We call it Rat Island!"

And so, to Rat Island or the Isle of Innisfree, they set out on a rough passage under lowering clouds, accompanied by a young priest who appeared from nowhere. She found no log cabin, no nine bean rows, or bee loud glade on the island, which was very small, but was covered with rowan trees. She determined to take some rowan branches back for Yeats and gathered a great armful. On the way back, the wind rose and the rain fell and the waves of the lake grew higher. She noticed that the priest, as white as a sheet, between one wave and the next was telling his rosary with one hand, and plucking off rowan berries with the other, to drop them in the water. Whether to invoke pagan as well as Christian divine aid was uncertain. Anyhow, it did not impress the boatman.

"Ah, Father," he said, "it's not the weight of a berry or two that will save us now!"

Once safely ashore, she caught the next Dublin train, and arrived soaked to the skin, and unannounced, at the house of the great poet, whom she had never met before, but who received her courteously; and of the friendship that subsequently developed she had this to say:

> These men – AE, Yeats, James Stephens, and the rest – had aristocratic minds. For them, the world was not fragmented. An idea did not suddenly grow, like Topsy, all alone and separate. For them, all things had antecedents, and long family trees. They saw nothing shameful or silly in myths and fairy stories, nor did they shovel them out of sight in some cupboard marked 'Only for Children'.

Which is very much what we have found to be the attitude and sentiments of Tolkien, who had his own problems with makers of films. One of the most amusing items in his *Collected Letters* is his response in 1958 to a proposed film treatment of *The Lord of the Rings* where he expostulates in no uncertain terms about the intrusion of a fairy castle, a great many eagles, not to mention incantations, blue lights, some irrelevant magic and a preference for fights over story line… and so it goes on for seven pages. This is long before the three-part version of the film directed by Peter Jackson, which I have to say certainly impressed me and I imagine might not have entirely displeased Tolkien himself.

And so the question remains as to whether film and television are suitable media for works of the deeper imagination. Those who doubt whether they are include C.S. Lewis, in his collection of essays *Of This and Other Worlds*. He argues that neither cinema nor television can replace popular fiction because they exclude precisely that which gives the untrained mind access to the imaginative world. That when it comes to stimulating the imagination, there is death in the camera.

Tolkien even had his reservations about the live theatre. And similar reservations have been expressed about pictorial illustration in books. I must say I am not too sure about all this, and as far as I am concerned, the jury is still out. Although I would say that I think that radio and audio media can be very good ways of expressing the imaginative tradition, and used sympathetically, can be a modern equivalent to the bard or minstrel telling the ancient lays around the communal fire. But best of all, of course, is the voice of the inspired story teller with a live group of people, be it esoteric workshop or children round a gifted teacher.

Another important point is the source of the imaginative material – which must be in the imagination of the prime creator, allowing the images to rise. This was certainly how C.S. Lewis and Tolkien worked. Lewis tells us that he was nagged for years by the recurrent image of a fawn carrying umbrella and parcels in a snowy wood. Eventually he followed it up and finished up with the seven volumes of *The Chronicles of Narnia*. Similarly J.R.R. Tolkien, whilst engaged upon a boring task of marking elementary examination papers, came upon the image and phrase "in a hole in the ground there lived a hobbit." In following this up to discover what a hobbit was he produced *The Lord of the Rings*. P.L. Travers insists that she did not contrive Mary Poppins, but simply that one day, parrot headed umbrella, carpet bag and all, she just flew into her life.

How can this kind of thing be coped with by organisations of mass entertainment? One example can be found in the form of a guide book called *The Writer's Journey, Mythic Structure for Storytellers and Screenwriters*. The author, Christopher Vogler, a dedicated professional if ever there was one, has apparently evaluated thousands of screenplays for the big motion picture studios. He provides a guide for plot structure and characterisation of the story line of the typical hero, based upon his understanding of the work of the mythologist Joseph Campbell.

I was interested to see, however, that between editions, on giving lectures further afield than Hollywood he had been confronted with some severe challenges to his universal panacea. Apart from a basic objection that such an analytical approach to the creative process was likely to lead to stale repetitious formula rather than to organic form he met with various accusations of cultural imperialism – American values and assumptions threatening to smother the unique flavours of other cultures. To say nothing of radical criticisms that questioned the role of the hero anyway, in terms of stemming from a warrior culture, to say nothing of problems of gender.

Vogler was straightforward enough to admit and to face up to these arguments and there is obviously food for considerable discussion in all of this in the field of cultural studies. In our more restricted field of the interface between the esoteric tradition and popular culture what interests me is the polar interchange between the particular and the universal. How the broad patterns of the cosmic and universal may be expressed in terms of any particular place and time. We can see this demonstrated to some degree by scanning the pages of an encyclopaedia of world mythology.

Another, slightly off beat angle on this, is, I think, to be found in the highly successful novels of Terry Pratchett. They are based on a fantasy world that he has made up, the Discworld – "flat, circular, and carried through space on the back of four elephants who in turn stand on the back of ... a turtle ten thousand miles long, dusted by the frost of dead comets, meteor-pocked, albedo-eyed. No-one knows the reason for all this, but it is probably quantum." Yet it is difficult to imagine this world being very far away in conceptual terms from traditional England – almost the England of Alfred Noyes in fact.

What is more, although Pratchett casts his net wide in terms of subject matter, there is a strong ambience of the esoteric within his world. This seems to me a most interesting cultural indicator. For it implies that the esoteric is nowadays sufficiently familiar for Pratchett's readers, who run to millions, to appreciate a comical and satirical treatment of it, and through which, moreover, some serious points are occasionally made. For, like Charles Williams and C.S. Lewis, whatever his personal attitude to the esoteric may be, Terry Pratchett certainly seems to know a fair bit about it.

We might take as an example his novel *Lords and Ladies*, the plot of which hangs around the conflict between some white witches and the elven powers behind a stone circle that some dabblers in the occult have inadvertently evoked. This could be serious stuff indeed, and in other hands, such as Dennis Wheatley or Charles Williams or C.S. Lewis or M.R. James. However with a mini-coven of traditional witches consisting of Granny Weatherwax, the much married Nanny Ogg, and Magrat Garlick "of the red nose and unkempt hair and tendency to be soppy about raindrops and roses and whiskers on kittens" we are projected into a world that is at once, more ridiculous, and yet at the same time more believable.

Certainly there seems something very familiar about the aspiring younger generation of new age witches Diamanda Tockley, Perdita Nitt and Amanita DeVice with their penchant for floppy black velvet hats, black painted finger nails, stark white make up, and dagger-and-skull tattoos, who, having done a bit of candle magic and some scrying, now fancy their chances of raising the power at a stone circle.

Owing to an odd combination of circumstances their evocation is more effective than they bargain for and a rather pushy elven Queen attempts to come through, who eventually gets her comeuppance from Granny Weatherwax and Nanny Ogg.

These two redoubtable heroines have no romantic illusions about the Faery Folk. They grant that they may be beautiful and glamorous beings but at the same time realise that they might have different ideas of behaviour from our own. Who might even smash the world if they thought it would make a pretty noise. Granny Weatherwax tends to class them with cats. "'Elves are beautiful. They've got," she spat the word, "*style*. Beauty. Grace. That's what matters. If cats looked like frogs we'd realize what nasty, cruel little bastards they are.'"

Let me say that I am, nonetheless, quite fond of cats, and even, for that matter of elves, but I think Granny Weatherwax has a point. With neither species does one take liberties – especially big cats. Lion taming, along with hobnobbing with the Fair Folk, the Gentry, the Shining Ones, the Star People is a somewhat specialist vocation, that is perhaps best left to the Robert Kirks and Thomas the Rhymers of this world.

However there is another side to it, as P.L. Travers records in her collection of reflections on myth, symbol and story, *What the Bee Knows*. When she met Laurens van der Post, he was fascinated by one element of Mary Poppins' accoutrements, her carpet bag. It reminded him of the story of a bushman who saw one night a crowd of beautiful girls coming down from the stars on a cord. Each one had a little basket and he caught one of them, who agreed to be his wife on condition that he never looked in the basket without her permission. Of course, as happens with all such prohibitions laid on from another world, one day he disobeyed the injunction and took a look inside, then he roared with laughter. His star maiden suspected what he had done and accused him of looking into her basket. He admitted it, and asked why she had made such a secret of it, because there was nothing in it. At this, she looked at him very sadly, and walked away into the sunset. Because he could not see all the wonders she had brought him from the stars.

Van der Post saw this as a parable of the way that the pundits, the intellectuals and critics look into the basket of star stuff and say it is all rubbish and superstition. That "there's nothing in it".

When Mary Poppins arrived at No. 17 Cherry Tree Lane and the children looked into her carpet bag they too thought it was empty. But they were lucky, Mary Poppins took it all in good part and did not walk away. Out of it came all her mundane possessions, a starched white apron, a large cake of Sunlight Soap, a toothbrush, a packet of hairpins, a bottle of scent, a small folding armchair, a box of throat lozenges, seven flannel night-gowns, four cotton ones, a pair of boots, a set of dominoes, two bathing-caps, a postcard album, a folding camp bed complete with blankets and eiderdown, and a bottle of medicine that tasted of whatever you liked best, all a foretaste of her magical powers. It was in effect another form of the cauldron of the goddess. The same that belonged to Keridwen and from which Gwion drank some drops, to be drawn, after a series of elemental transformations, into union with the goddess, after which he was reborn as a bard and poet – Taliesin.

Which all goes to show that the esoteric tradition is where you find it, even in the most unlikely or popular of places.

But we cannot part tonight without a thought towards our founder Kathleen Raine, who conceived the idea for this series of talks and who was sat here just before me when I gave the first of them. I recall that, as an example of those who could see nothing in the star lady's basket she was fond of castigating Dr Johnson who felt he had refuted idealistic philosophy simply by kicking a stone.

This reminds me of some remarks of Thomas Carlyle, who was called the Sage of Chelsea, much as Kathleen might be regarded as the Guardian of Ancient Springs in much the same location. Here is what he had to say in regard to Dr Johnson and his attitude toward ghosts.

> The English Johnson longed, all his life, to see one; but could not, though he went to Cock Lane, and thence to the church vaults, and tapped on coffins. Foolish Doctor! Did he never, with the mind's eye as with the body's, look round him into that full tide of human Life he so loved; did he never so much as look into Himself? The good Doctor was a Ghost, as actual and authentic as heart could wish; well nigh a million of Ghosts were travelling the streets by his side…Are we not Spirits, that are shaped into a body, into an Appearance; and that fade away again into air and Invisibility? This is no metaphor, it is a simple scientific fact; we start out of Nothingness, take figure, and are Apparitions; round us, as round the veriest spectre, is Eternity.

And so, my fellow embodied ghosts, gathered here tonight in this place, and in Eternity, I would close by invoking, through the words of Carlyle, a realisation of the continuing fellowship with our friend and mentor Kathleen Raine:

> Is the lost Friend still mysteriously Here, even as we are Here mysteriously, with God? Know of a truth that only the Time-shadows have perished, or are perishable. That the real Being of whatever was, and whatever is, and whatever will be, is even now and forever.
>
> This, should it unhappily seem new, thou mayest ponder at thy leisure, for the next twenty years or the next twenty centuries. **Believe** it thou **must**; **understand** it thou canst **not!**

THE DWELLER ON THE THRESHOLD

THE DWELLER on the Threshold is a menacing figure that is described by a number of leading esoteric teachers, not only Madame Blavatsky in her monumental *Isis Unveiled* and Rudolf Steiner in his *Knowledge of the Higher Worlds* but also Dion Fortune in her fiction and non-fiction. Firstly in *The Scented Poppies*, one of the stories in *The Secrets of Dr. Taverner* and later in her principal text book *The Mystical Qabalah*.

Although the concept may have been a reality of esoteric initiation from ancient times, we owe the term itself, with certain minor variants, to the 19th century novelist Edward Bulwer-Lytton and his famous occult novel *Zanoni* of 1842.

Bulwer-Lytton, (1803-73) was a scion of one of England's stately homes that remains open to the public: Knebsworth, 29 miles north of London, near Stevenage. He was a pioneer historical novelist, and far more meticulous in his research and accurate in his facts than his contemporaries Sir Walter Scott or Harrison Ainsworth; his principal works in this genre including *Harold, the last of the Saxon Kings*, *The Last of the Barons* and *The Last Days of Pompeii*. He was also a successful politician, being Secretary of State for the Colonies in 1858, and for his achievements as a novelist, playwright and statesman was raised to the peerage in 1866.

He was also very knowledgeable in what we nowadays call the Western Esoteric Tradition, and it is said that the famous French occultist Eliphas Lévi came to England to visit him, although the tradition of secrecy that veiled these matters in those days was such that it is difficult to ascertain the cause of their meeting or what may have happened as a consequence. However, many a true word is revealed in fiction, and so it is worth our while to seek what Lytton may have revealed in his occult novel, particularly in light of a few portentous hints that he drops in its Introduction.

In reading one of his novels we have to adjust our minds to the fact that it is written in the elaborate and somewhat mannered style of a bygone age, and so may seem a trifle long winded and overblown to the modern reader. But it is worth persisting to make the necessary mental adjustment. It is to no great credit of a minor American University that considers it a great jape to have hailed Bulwer-Lytton as the worst novelist in the English language and to award prizes for examples of turgid and verbose prose – a display of academic philistinism that serves only to demonstrate their own lack of historical sense in terms of style. Indeed some of Bulwer-Lytton's lines have an evocative ring, and are unconsciously quoted by many people even to this day. Not least is the opening of one of his other novels: "It was a dark and stormy night…" to say nothing of "the pen is mightier than the sword."

Edward Bulwer-Lytton

The Introductory chapter to the story of *Zanoni* recounts how the narrator, in his younger days, had been keen to become acquainted with the true origin and tenets of the Rosicrucians. In his search he frequented an obscure bookshop in Covent Garden, where he met an old man who hinted that he might well enlighten him should they happen to meet again. Indeed they do so meet very shortly afterwards at the foot of Highgate Hill and the old man invites the young man to his house, in a secluded part of Highgate overlooking London, and instructs him in esoteric philosophy.

He tells that the Rosicrucians still exist, but pursue their profound researches into natural science and occult philosophy in august secrecy. Yet however respectable and virtuous they might be, and ardent in the Christian faith, they are but a branch of another more transcendent, powerful and illustrious Order that derives from Plato, Pythagoras and Apollonius of Tyana.

On his death, the old man bequeaths to the narrator a manuscript in cipher, which turns out to be the text of the novel *Zanoni*. It is described by its anonymous author as a romance and yet not a romance. As a source of truth for those who can understand it, but a wild extravaganza for those who cannot. And so with this in mind we may well profit from examining the novel for its hidden truth.

The old man, referring to the works of Plato, has already explained that there are four stages for the soul in its return to its first state of happiness in God. The first is music, the second mysticism, the third prophecy, and the fourth love. And it is upon this outline plan that the story of *Zanoni* is constructed.

The novel divides into seven parts, which are entitled:
1. *The Musician*
2. *Art, Love and Wonder*
3. *Theurgia*
4. *The Dweller of the Threshold*
5. *The Effects of the Elexir*
6. *Superstition Deserting Faith*
7. *The Reign of Terror.*

This last section is an evocation of the French Revolution, along with Bulwer-Lytton's close adherence to fact, in which the occult adept Zanoni goes voluntarily to his sacrificial death in an attempt to save the innocent from the guillotine.

His death is of considerable philosophical importance, for Zanoni is no ordinary mortal. He was born a star and fire worshipper in ancient Chaldea, and so is some 4000 years old, his occult powers having enabled him to avoid the ravages of time. He is one of only two members of a great ancient esoteric Order who survive. The other initiate is named Mejnour and he, choosing a different path from Zanoni, may presumably still be living to this day. Whilst all this may sound fantastic, the esoteric status of Zanoni and Mejnour is much akin to that which is accorded by latter day occultists to Masters of the Wisdom, and what Lytton has to say about these Adepti pre-dates by some forty years the celebrated Mahatamas of Madame Blavatsky or the Secret Chiefs of the Golden Dawn.

The heroine of the novel is Viola, a young Neapolitan girl, ignorant and uneducated but a supremely gifted singer. Its hero Zanoni, the master of mystic and prophetic arts, loves her for her youth, innocence and musical gifts. His co-initiate Mejnour remains wedded to the pursuit of knowledge for its own sake – looking upon human love as a weakness rather than a strength.

Having helped Viola to become a star of the Neopolitan opera, Zanoni, although he loves her, tries to divert her natural love for him by encouraging her courtship by a young Englishman, Glyndon. His grounds for this are that he, being virtually an immortal, cannot realistically form a lasting loving relationship with a young girl who will grow old, wither and die in the natural course of life, whilst he himself remains relatively unaffected by the passage of time.

His selfless plans are aborted by the young Englishman, an amateur artist of some talent but of solid respectable middle class stock, who cannot come to terms with taking a poor Italian girl for wife. How would she fit in on the English social scene? How would she be received by his parents or by his business associates? He hankers instead after the mysterious powers of Mejnour and Zanoni.

After some heart searching by all concerned, Glyndon is eventually accepted for initiatory instruction under the adept Mejnour at a hidden temple in the mountains. In the meantime

The Dweller on the Threshold

Zanoni marries Viola, hoping that perhaps he may be able to instruct her sufficiently in his secret sciences so that she too may avoid the march of time. Both these schemes founder in the test of hard reality and human fallibility.

Glyndon, although spurred on in his mystic quest by having an alchemist as a distant ancestor, proves himself to be lacking in the qualities required of an initiate. The Dweller on the Threshold proves too much for him. He cannot resist the lure of idle curiosity or the temptations of the flesh – tests that have been arranged by Mejnour. He is accordingly rejected and returned to the world, but having evoked the wind he reaps the whirlwind, and undergoes a slow moral degeneration. This manifests at first as drunken self indulgence and social ineptitude, and passes in the end to lust and treachery.

Viola, on the other hand, the simple Neapolitan girl, is disastrously influenced by the local priest, who condemns her involvement with a man who practices the occult arts. Despite the exemplary conduct of her husband she begins to fear his knowledge and his background, and refuses all thought of him teaching her any of his esoteric powers. So fearful does she become, for their child as much as herself, that she deserts Zanoni – an instance of what is described as "superstition deserting faith" in Bulwer-Lytton's section headings – the superstition of the ignorant priest over the faith in her wise and loving husband. By force of circumstances she ends up in Paris at the time of the worst excesses of the Revolution. Here, partly through the perfidy of Glyndon, she is denounced and condemned to the guillotine. Zanoni arrives and, in a desperate attempt to save her, sacrifices his own life in the process but goes to his death with a new realisation of the meaning of human life, and above all of human death. Despite his efforts, by a quirk of fate, Viola also dies, and their child is left an orphan in the prison cell, although the book ends with the strong hint that he will grow up safely as "the fatherless are in the care of God".

Throughout all these colourful events the author stresses the theme of the quest of the ideal in the arts, as opposed to the servile imitation of nature, for nature is not to be copied but exalted. The aim of the arts should be to lift the perceptions of the beholder to the level of the gods, to the highest potential of mankind.

Yet the natural world is not to be rejected. Man's spirit is like a bird and cannot always be on the wing. They who best evoke the ideal also enjoy the most real. For true art finds beauty everywhere, in the street, the market place, or the hovel. Exemplary models are Shakespeare, Raphael, the sculptors of classical Greece. Milton and Dante found inspiration for their song even in the mire of politics.

As to the powers of the mind, expressed in wisdom or prophecy, whoever can perceive the truths that are in him and around him can foretell what is likely to come. But the perception of truth is disturbed by many inner causes – vanity, passion, fear, indolence, ignorance. It is only a particular state of mind – of profound serenity – that is capable of perceiving truth.

Glyndon, although seeking for higher truth, has a mind that is fevered by a desire for it. He seeks the deepest secrets in nature without trial or preparation of himself. Yet truth cannot be seen by the mind that is unprepared for it. Such a mind receives truth only to pollute it. In the words of the neo-platonist Iamblichus: "He who pours water into a muddy well, only disturbs the mud."

Nor is this is simply a matter of stirring up unresolved subconscious complexes as modern psychological analysts might have us believe; it has an objective side to it as well. Citing Bulwer-Lytton's *Zanoni*, Madame Blavatsky, in *Isis Unveiled*, refers to the Dweller on the Threshold in the plural, as beings, some of them vicious, who surround us and move in the astral waves like fish in the water. Such astral currents can be controlled only by an adept, pure in mind and spirit, who knows how to direct these blind forces.

She asserts that Bulwer-Lytton is the only author in the world of literature to give such a truthful and evocative description of these astral beings, quoting directly from the adept Mejnour instructing the aspiring Glyndon:

> Man is arrogant in proportion to his ignorance. For several ages he saw in the countless worlds that sparkle through space like the bubbles of a shoreless ocean, only the petty candles ... that Providence has been pleased

to light for no other purpose but to make the night more agreeable to man … Astronomy has corrected this delusion of human vanity, and man now reluctantly confesses that the stars are worlds, larger and more glorious than his own … Everywhere, then, in this immense design, science brings new life to light … Reasoning, then, by evident analogy, if not a leaf, if not a drop of water, but is, no less than yonder star, a habitable and breathing world – nay, if even man himself, is a world to other lives, and millions and myriads dwell in the rivers of his blood, and inhabit man's frame, as man inhabits earth – common sense (if our schoolmen had it) would suffice to teach that the circumfluent infinite which you call space – that boundless impalpable which divides earth from the moon and stars – is filled also with its correspondent and appropriate life.

Is it not a visible absurdity to suppose that being is crowded upon every leaf, and yet absent from the immensities of space! The law of the great system forbids the waste even of an atom; it knows no spot where something of life does not breathe … Well, then, can you conceive that space, which is infinite itself, is alone a waste, is alone lifeless, is less useful to the one design of universal being … than the peopled leaf, than the swarming globule? The microscope shows you the creatures on the leaf; no mechanical tube is yet invented to discover the nobler and more gifted things that hover in the illimitable air. Yet between these last and man is a mysterious and terrible affinity …

But first, to penetrate this barrier, the soul with which you listen must be sharpened by intense enthusiasm, purified from all earthly desires … When thus prepared, science can be brought to aid it; the sight itself may be rendered more subtile, the nerves more acute, the spirit more alive and outward, and the element itself – the air, the space – may be made, by certain secrets of the higher chemistry, more palpable and clear. And this, too, is not magic as the credulous call it; as I have so often said before, magic (a science that violates nature) exists not; it is but the science by which nature can be controlled. Now in space there are millions of beings, not literally spiritual, for they have all, like the animalcula unseen by the naked eye, certain forms of matter, though matter is so delicate, air-drawn, and subtile, that it is, as it were, but a film, a gossamer, that clothes the spirit … Yet, in truth, these races differ most widely … some surpassing wisdom, some of horrible malignity; some hostile as fiends to men, others gentle as messengers between earth and heaven ... Amid the dwellers on the threshold is one, too, surpassing in malignity and hatred all her tribe; one whose eyes have paralyzed the bravest, and whose power increases over the spirit precisely in proportion to its fear.

Such, says Madame Blavatsky, is a sketch of elemental beings void of divine spirit, given by one whom many with reason believed to know more than he was prepared to admit in the face of an incredulous public.

She returns to the subject with reference to psychic phenomena, which can be subjective or objective – a distinction which we must ever bear in mind.

"An impure medium," she says, "will attract to his impure inner self, the vicious, depraved, malignant influences as inevitably as one that is pure draws only those that are good and pure." And she cites as one of the latter kind, a contemporary, Baroness Adelma von Vay, who used her mediumistic powers to heal the sick and comfort the afflicted, and who for many years had seen and recognised nature spirits and cosmic elementaries and found them always friendly.

Others, less pure and good, had not fared so well at the hands of these apish and impish beings. And although spiritualists might not believe in their existence, these nature spirits are nonetheless realities. Bulwer-Lytton's Dwellers might be a modern conception but the idea derives from ancient Hebraic and Egyptian tradition. Orthodox Christians might call them devils, or imps of Satan, and the like, but they are nothing of the kind. They are simply creatures of ethereal matter, irresponsible, neither good nor bad, unless influenced by a superior intelligence. Such was known by one of the early church fathers, Clement of Alexandria, who remarked that it was absurd to call them devils for they were only inferior angels, "powers which inhabit elements, move the winds and distribute showers, and as such are agents and subject to God."

A further reference to their role in psychic phenomena occurs in early Theosophical literature in one of *The Mahatma Letters to A.P. Sinnett*. This was in connection with some slighting references to *Zanoni* that had been made by Stainton Moses, a leading spiritualist of the day.

The Dweller on the Threshold

Stainton Moses was no ordinary medium. A public school master and ordained minister, he began to experience trances which were accompanied by startling physical phenomena, from which emerged a sequence of spiritual teaching from a being known as Imperator. The tone of the teachings were of a neo-platonic nature and somewhat at variance with the Reverend Stainton Moses' initial more orthodox Christian beliefs. In the early days of the Theosophical Society, Madame Blavatsky had looked upon Stainton Moses as a possible important ally in her struggle against the forces of nineteenth century materialism. However, a rift gradually began to emerge between them regarding the comparative status of Imperator on the one hand and her Masters Morya and Koot Hoomi on the other.

This all too human controversy began to generate more heat than light, although it centred upon a fundamental question that is perennial to all occultism, as to exactly who Masters, Inner Plane Adepti or Spirit Teachers are, their spiritual status and the nature of their being. Contemporaneously, Anna Kingsford was promulgating *The Perfect Way* in which she asserted that the source of such teachings was the Higher Self of each one involved, and was reluctant to admit credence or superiority to Imperator or the Theosophical Mahatamas alike. Be this as it may, it is of interest that there were three independent major influxes of teaching of this nature during the early 1880s.

As to the nature of the Dweller on the Threshold, Stainton Moses, who had also read Bulwer-Lytton, was inclined to be somewhat sceptical. Indeed he asked Madame Blavatsky if she thought Bulwer-Lytton's description of this being had been the result of the author's dreams after eating underdone pork chops! To this the old lady had prophesied that in a year's time he might have to face and fight the same thing. And sure enough thirteen months later he wrote her to say:

> "I am fighting a hand to hand battle with all the legions of the Fiend for the past three weeks. My nights are made hideous with their torments, temptations and foul suggestions. I see them all around, glaring at me,

gabbling, howling, grinning! Every form of filthy suggestion, of bewildering doubt, of mad and shuddering fear is upon me ... I have not wavered yet ... and their temptations are fainter, the presence less near, the horror less..."

In a letter received by A.P. Sinnett in July 1881, Koot Hoomi analyses the reasons for this and claims all would have been well if Moses had asserted his own independent spiritual will by giving up mediumship. Imperator, he says, cannot preach the occult sciences and then defend mediumship, for mediumship is abnormal. It may represent a stage on the way in certain cases, (and we should recall that both Blavatsky and Dion Fortune were mediums in their time), but when by further development the abnormal has given way to the natural, spirit controls are shaken off, along with passive obedience. The medium learns to use his or her own will, to exercise his or her own power, to become an adept. The process is one of development and no initiate who is subject to trance can truly be called an adept.

The progress of the initiate upon the Path is taken up by Rudolf Steiner in his textbook *Knowledge of the Higher Worlds – How is it Achieved?*, first published in 1909/10 as *The Way of Initiation* and *Initiation and its Results*. The book culminates with two chapters describing the meeting of the Dweller on the Threshold, virtually as the end result of the initiation process. He prefers to use the term Guardian (or at any rate his translators do) although he undoubtedly has Bulwer-Lytton's *Zanoni* in mind.

He describes the process as being in two parts, as there are two Thresholds, a Lesser and a Greater, each with its correspondent Guardian, and he writes that although descriptions sometimes given are enough to make timid souls shudder, dangers only exist if the necessary precautions are neglected. If a valid course of esoteric training is pursued then the ascent will proceed through experiences of increasing power and magnitude with no question of injury to health or life.

Such a course of training entails a sense of participation in the physical as well as the spiritual worlds, for the Earth is transformed by the initiate implanting within it what he or she discovers in the spiritual world, for the physical Earth is dependent upon the spiritual world. And anyone seeking to shirk the tasks of the outer world by escaping into another world will never reach the goal of initiation.

Until the soul crosses the first Threshold it has been directed and controlled by external forces of destiny, or karma, according to its deserts, good or bad. Crossing the first threshold is a taking of full responsibility for one's own actions.

In one sense this means becoming free from the forces of karma, as externally applied, but it also implies becoming aware of one's own true state of being (in conjunction with the Delphic oracle's adage to "Know Thyself") and to take responsibility for it. The Dweller in this instance is a mirror image of the soul, warts and all, but rather than being fearful of it the initiate at this stage should take responsibility for its transformation or redemption.

Here, in an interesting footnote, Steiner remarks that the Guardian, being an astral figure, could be made physically visible by an operation of lower magic, producing, by whatever means, a cloud of fine substance which may be moulded into the form and vitalised by the unresolved karma of the individual concerned. However, such operations are not to be recommended as they bring with them the risk of falling into evil byways. He cites Bulwer-Lytton's novel *Zanoni* as containing a description of such an operation in fictional form. This is when Mejnour lays on a demonstration of spirits for Glyndon, which forms part of his test of obedience to his teacher and resistance to idle curiosity, and seems in some respects closely akin to the physical phenomena of certain spiritualist circles and which habitually manifested about Stainton Moses.

One consequence of passing the first Threshold is a realisation of the existence of group souls, national souls, folk angels, the ancestors – and that the individual is part and parcel of a number of greater beings of the supersensual worlds. At the same time there will come about a different attitude towards death, for after crossing this threshold the initiate becomes as a living dead man – a point also made in Dion Fortune's *The Cosmic Doctrine* – macabre as this might seem to the 'once born', the ordinary personality in the world that has not yet been opened up to higher consciousness.

The second Threshold leads on to a cosmic landscape and the initiate becomes a citizen of the higher worlds beyond the trammels of the flesh and the physical world. In one sense this corresponds to the initiation of Daath upon the Tree of Life, beyond which are the Supernal or Formless Worlds, and some further hints about its possibilities may be found in *The Rays and the Initiations* by Alice A. Bailey, which builds in some detail upon some outline hints first given in Blavatsky's *The Secret Doctrine*.

Our first concern however will be with the meeting with the first Dweller. In chapter 21 of *The Mystical Qabalah* Dion Fortune describes it somewhat ominously as a horror which confronts every adventurer into the Unseen, although her ensuing analysis of it makes clear that much depends upon our own psychological and philosophical preparation for it. That is to say, our realisation of just exactly what we are doing or seeking to achieve when we seek initiation.

In her eyes, in this function it unites in itself the functions of the Sphinx, presenting a riddle to the soul upon the answer to which hangs its fate, either returned to wander in the realms of illusion or permitted to pass on into the Light. This riddle of the Sphinx is, 'Do you believe in the gods?'

If the initiate answers 'Yes' or 'No' then he or she will remain a wanderer in the planes of illusion, for the gods are not real persons as we understand personality, yet nor, on the other hand, are they illusions. What then shall be the answer?

In search of this, Dion Fortune enters into an analysis of the nature of what Theosophists call the Akasha, or western occultists such as Eliphas Lévi the Reflecting Ether. This may seem to make the Dweller or Guardian more of a philosophical problem than a grisly horror, but upon the successful resolution of it depends the future progress of the initiate, who stands at the threshold of a three-fold way. One way is to continue to wander in the illusory world of superstition and psychic self deception; the second is to abandon the inner quest and return to more materialist speculations (which include various forms of psychology, whatever the transcendental veneer of some of them); the third way leads to the opening up of higher consciousness in the objective realms of the Unseen.

In what we have seen so far, the various approaches of Bulwer-Lytton, Blavatsky, Steiner and Dion Fortune to the Dweller, or Guardian, on or of the Threshold, reflect different facets of this stage of the initiatory progress of the soul. In Eastern terms it might be described as an image, or indeed personification, of the karmic debit account. In traditional Christian terms it might be regarded as a vista of Purgatory, whilst in Ancient Egyptian imagery it might be seen as the weighing of the soul in the ante-chamber of Osiris. All these are descriptions of an after death condition, which may however be experienced in life by the process of initiation.

The approach to the Dweller, it might be said, is a gradual one. It is only to be feared if the meeting is premature, a result of vaulting spiritual ambition, as in the case of Glyndon in the story of *Zanoni*. In real life the consequences are hardly likely to be so immediate and dramatic as those described in the Dr Taverner story, *The Scented Poppies*.

Here Dion Fortune achieves a striking finish when a budding occultist, who is also a singularly nasty piece of work, at his own presumptuous request has his psychic faculties prematurely opened for him by Dr. Taverner. He is immediately confronted with the horrifying vision of the shadow side of his own soul, which Taverner casually refers to as the Guardian of the Threshold. As a result, the man runs screaming into the night – although the story omits to say whether it was "a dark and stormy" one! And fortunately, it has to be said, this is not the usual result of an esoteric initiation.

However, as in most approaches to the unseen worlds, it is the manner of our approach to it that governs its response to us. Hence the emphasis upon right motive at the threshold of any responsible occult school.

JOURNEY TO THE MOON

THE TREE of Life of the Qabalah is an invaluable comprehensive glyph upon which much of the Western Esoteric Tradition is based, for by its means it is possible to classify and compare many symbols from a variety of mythological, religious and philosophical systems.

In its system of interrelated spheres it represents ten aspects of the emanations of God, from Fount of Creation in the Highest Heaven, to the Holy Presence on Earth as the Shekinah. As such it is a very holy device for the worship and understanding of God by Hebrew mystics, whilst to the occultist of the Western Esoteric Tradition it is also a metaphysical route map of the inner planes.

Between the ten spheres are twenty two interconnecting paths and it is the symbols associated with each of these paths that provide keys to mystical and occult experience, or in a more subjective mode, to psychological analysis with a metaphysical and spiritual dimension.

The general method of working with the symbols of the Paths is to visualise going upon a journey along the Path and meeting three key images on the way. Starting at a location that symbolically represents the Sphere of departure, we are confronted by a Tarot trump, regarded as a picture or veil through which we have to pass. Then midway down the Path we come upon a key point which is illuminated or overshadowed by the configuration of the Hebrew letter, and its various associations. Finally at the end of the Path we come to an astronomical body or constellation that stands before the Sphere of our destination. The Spheres of commencement and achievement, or Sephiroth, represent conditions of consciousness;

so in treading the Path we should have processed from one mode of consciousness to another.

Plainly, with twenty-two Paths and ten Sephiroth, the field that opens before us is potentially a vast one, but by way of illustration let us concentrate upon the first one that confronts us, the so-called 32nd Path that leads from Malkuth (the Kingdom) to Yesod (the Foundation), or ordinary consciousness of the physical world around us, or Earth consciousness, to the first level of psychic perception, symbolically represented by the Moon and poetically described as the mistress of tides not only within the objective but within the subjective sphere.

Dion Fortune has evoked it well in one of her novels, *The Sea Priestess*, as the protagonist of her story sinks towards subconscious mentation while lying, partly drugged by medication for asthma, looking at the moonrise through his bedroom window:

> Now I cannot tell what I said to the Moon, or what the Moon said to me, but all the same, I got to know her very well. And this was the impression I got of her – that she ruled over a kingdom that was neither material nor spiritual, but a strange moon-kingdom all of her own. In it moved tides – ebbing, flowing, slack water, high water, never ceasing, always on the move; up and down, backwards and forwards, rising and receding; coming past on the flood, flowing back on the ebb; and these tides affected our lives. They affected birth and death and all the processes of the body. They affected the mating of animals, and the growth of vegetation, and the insidious workings of disease. They also affected the reactions of drugs, and there was a lore of herbs belonging to them. All these things I got by communing with the Moon, and I felt certain that if I could only learn the rhythm and periodicity of her tides I should know a very great deal.

The treading in visualisation of the 32nd Path should therefore be another way of approaching, in controlled higher consciousness, (not induced by drugs or illness), this inner world behind sensory consciousness.

In trying to describe the nature of the 32nd Path I do not think I can improve upon what I wrote some sixty years ago, in *A Practical Guide to Qabalistic Symbolism*:

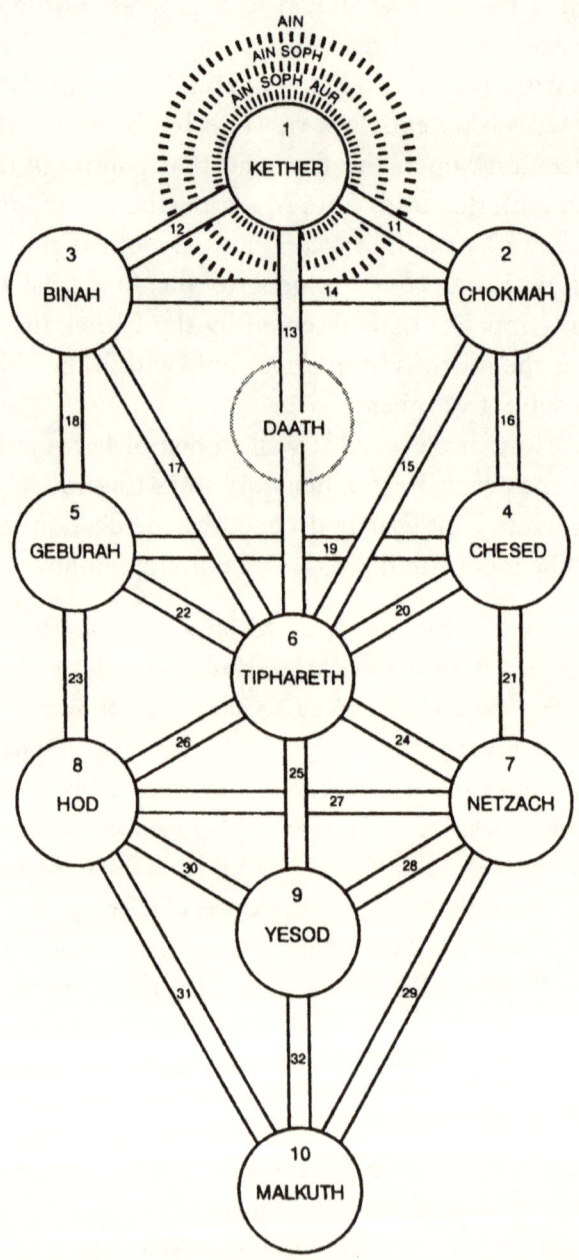

Qabalistic Tree of Life. The 32nd Path joins Malkuth to Yesod.

Journey to the Moon

This Path joins Malkuth, the physical world, and Yesod, the universal unconscious and etheric web which forms the foundation of physical existence. It is therefore a Path of introversion from the sensory consciousness to the consciousness of the deeps of the inner world. When one treads it one is boring down into the unconscious mind, and many and strange are the things that one may meet there.

It is like the hole in the earth into which Alice fell, leading to her strange adventures in Wonderland. It is also, on a mythological level, the way down to the Underworld, trod by Oedipus at Colonos, Orpheus in search of Eurydice and many others, but primarily it is Persephone's descent into the world of Pluto, the King of the Underworld. Alice, indeed, might be said to be a modern version of Persephone, for Carroll was a writer who wrote of the deeps of the unconscious mind.

The Path is also the way of psychoanalysis and shows the difference between the Freudian and Jungian techniques, for when the unconscious images of Yesod are met with, the Freudian tries to analyse them with reference to life history in Malkuth, daily living, but the Jungian process follows the images through until they become symbols of transformation leading to the psychic harmony of Tiphareth. In other words, the Jungian technique is, or should be, a pressing on to the 25th Path, Yesod-Tiphareth, after the way in, the 32nd Path, Malkuth-Yesod, has been trodden.

Indeed that further progression beyond the subconscious sphere of Yesod could be equated with the eventual revelation of the Jungian archetype of the Self, in Tiphareth. However, we should also be prepared to realise that this is not merely a subjective world, but that it has an objective side to it.

However, let us take but one step – or one Path – at a time, to make the method of progress clear. The symbols on this Path, according to the most generally accepted tradition in modern occultism, are Tarot Trump XXI, the World; the Hebrew letter Tau; and the planet Saturn.

A lot depends upon how we formulate and meet up with the bare bones of the basic symbolism, for allowing the images to rise, with their relevant associations, is the secret of practical magical work. Whilst the main symbols are subject to convention there are various ways in which they may be met or presented, and to illustrate this we can examine three practical examples culled from different practitioners – which may help to give us more flexibility in our own personal approach.

The convention is to start within a visualised location that is usually in the form of a simple temple, thus providing a spiritualised ambience to what is to take place, placing it somewhat above the personal psychological concerns of everyday life.

In the first example we find ourselves in the Temple of Malkuth in the form of a circular space surrounded by a grove of black pillars shot with gold, with a black and white chequered paving between them. In the centre is an altar in the form of a double cube, a light upon it, the flame of which extends upwards into an angelic form in the Elemental colours of citrine, olive, russet and black – that of the Archangel Sandalphon, who oversees the planet Earth.

Upon the eastern side of the temple three doors are to be seen, although it is only the central one that concerns us. It is veiled by a curtain upon which is depicted the Tarot trump of The World – a great oval wreath of laurels intertwined with lilies and roses, about which are the four conventional figures of a bull, a lion, a man and an eagle, whilst within the dark oval within the wreath is a pale naked hermaphroditic figure, seen to be approaching from a great distance, holding two spirals, one in each hand, of silver and of gold. The figure indicates that we follow and we visualise ourselves passing through the wreath, into the picture.

The situation becomes three dimensional as we find ourselves floating in a deep indigo mist. It has the feeling that it might be the bottom of an ocean, and as we realise this so we begin to feel sand beneath our feet, with rocky and uneven surfaces, dark slippery weed, and various fish-like creatures swimming round about us.

As we proceed, the way before us seems to get a little lighter and we see that there is a giant figure approaching. He appears to be lame and has a large staff which he is uses as a kind of crutch. He is about six or seven feet tall and seemingly Greek, and thus might be

Oedipus – he who answered the riddle of the sphinx – or possibly it could be the healing god Asclepius.

He is waiting for us, and as we approach he looks at us searchingly. Then he turns and limps off before us as our guide. The way we are going now seems to be more of a defined path until we come to what might be called a glade on the sea bed, although in place of trees there are great walls of weed trailing upwards, with dark shadows all around, but in the centre, above us shining in golden light, is the Hebrew letter of the Path, Tau (ת). The club-footed shape of one of the two down strokes of this letter bears a certain resonance with the great limping figure who is custodian of this glade.

We pass on, however, and as we go we begin to feel that we are losing our weight. We are becoming less dense and beginning to float upwards. As we do so, the dark indigo sea begins to become brighter, almost a Mediterranean blue, and we find we are about to break the surface of the ocean, and we rise above the surface of the sea. In the sky, huge above us, is a close up view of the planet Saturn with its disc-shaped rings and several moons.

Below it, we see before us a long, low black barge – one imagines somewhat like the legendary barge which came to take the wounded King Arthur off to Avalon. It comes to rest before us and a great tall figure in the boat indicates we join him, and so we take our places on the plank seats within. He is robed in purple, and, strange as it may seem in a deep sea, holds a long pole by which he is punting us along over the still surface of the sea, beneath a starry sky in which the great planetary figure of Saturn is most prominent.

We now find we are approaching an island. It is of a grey kind of volcanic rock, and dominating it is a building of nine sides. As we watch, the building and the whole island begins to glow, and then to become translucent so that we can see through and inside it. Within we can see, seated upon a throne, a great female figure, of heavy and ponderous build and white pallor of skin, surrounded by maidens. She appears to be a goddess of the Moon.

She holds up her hand in recognition and salutation to us and we remain contemplating this figure, to see if any realisations come to mind, be it in the form of words or pictures or ideas.

This is the furthest extent of our journey, towards the fringes of Yesod, and having gleaned what we can from this contact, we proceed in a reverse direction, following the association of ideas and images back to whence we came. Via the boat propelled by the tall figure, who we begin to associate with the archangel of Yesod and of Annunciation, the Archangel Gabriel. Back to the point in the ocean where we broke the surface, down through the darkening waters to the glade containing the golden letter Tau, saluting the great lame figure as we pass, and thence back to and through the Tarot picture, through the wreath and into the visualised place from whence we started.

On a cursory reading this may not seem to have been a particularly significant experience, but it is another thing to proceed through the images slowly in a contemplative frame of mind, when the feeling will be that although it appeared to be just fanciful imaginings, yet somehow we have partaken of something real, that we feel we have 'been somewhere'.

This technique, that is known in some circles as 'initiated symbol projection', need not be confined to Qabalistic symbolism, but the Qabalistic system provides a comprehensive street map, so to speak, of the interior city of the soul, with its ten spheres and twenty two interconnecting paths.

Let us see how the same journey was undertaken by another guide, Charles Fielding in *The Practical Qabalah* (1991). This time we begin with the impression that we are deep within the Earth, in a large cave with rock walls and beaten earth floor. The cave is in a rough cube shape and in the centre is a square cut granite altar upon which is an ancient stone lamp, whose light is reflected in the facets of a piece of rock crystal resting in an unglazed dish beside it.

At the eastern wall is a curiously carved ancient wooden throne, behind which is a tapestry upon which is the life-sized figure of a dancing woman, naked apart from a wind-blown veil that covers her thighs, carrying two spiral rods, that twist in opposite directions, all within an oval wreath of laurel leaves. At the corners, as on the Tarot trump of The World, are the heads of a man, an eagle, a lion and a bull. This picture has an ambience of great reality.

Then the light in the cavern grows brighter and the flame upon the altar grows in size surrounded by many motes of intense multi-coloured light. These are the 'souls of fire', inner energies behind the physical world, and as the flame rises up the roof of the cave disappears to reveal the night sky with the seven stars of the Great Bear prominent, and the flame itself seeming to make a kind of fusion with the pole star, Polaris. This heralds an awareness of an angelic presence, Sandalphon, the traditional archangel of Malkuth.

We proceed to pass through the picture upon the eastern wall, which seems to be made of many lines of light something after the fashion of a television picture, and after a faint impression of passing through an archway, we find ourselves upon the other side, feeling more alive, lighter in body and clearer in mind, as if we have passed through some sieve or filter that prevents our grosser elements from coming with us.

The way ahead is dark but the way is illuminated to a certain extent by a faint greyish misty light emanated by our own bodies. A smooth rock path leads downward and becomes steeper, and rougher, even with dangerously loose scree. It also becomes narrower so that the indigo sky above becomes a mere narrow slit. Eventually the path flattens out and widens and gives onto a small plateau consisting of a sparse grove of ivy-covered oak trees and a feeling of great age. In the centre is a tall single cypress tree, shining silver white in a light that shines down from directly above it.

Some vast silent presence begins to make itself felt as spirit of this place. Past, present and future seem to coalesce as one and we see the light above to emanate from a Hebrew letter Tau burning with a soft white radiance.

Moving on, the path leading on from the plateau slopes gently downwards and the sky above is once again filled with stars, until the path levels off and then gently rises towards a low ridge, its dark crest rimmed with faint silver light. Moving slowly up toward this crest we see for a moment a figure of the ancient god Saturn, looking rather like Old Father Time with his scythe, who vanishes however as we reach the top.

We find we are standing looking over a lake beyond the ground that falls away before us, and over a small rocky islet in the lake there hangs a crescent moon. Upon the island is a nine-sided temple of Yesod seemingly made of crystal, shining with a violet radiance, encompassed by the aura of the great archangelic figure of Gabriel, whose wings fills the sky before us.

Having taken time to register this contact we then retrace our steps by the way we have come until we reach the place of our starting.

Finally turning to a third guide, Dolores Ashcroft-Nowicki in *The Shining Paths* (1983), we commence our journey in a somewhat more ornate version of the temple of Malkuth than hitherto. It is once again square, with black and white paving, but has a stained glass window at each side representing a winged bull, a winged lion, an eagle and a winged man or angel. In the centre is a black polished wood altar in the form of a double cube (that is, its height is twice the dimensions of its square top). Upon it is a light in a bowl of deep blue crystal, standing upon an altar cloth of linen scattered with ears of wheat.

There is also a pair of pillars, one of ebony and one of silver towards the east, before three ornate doors, before which there stands Sandalphon, a somewhat Dionysian figure in the appearance of a young man with dark curling hair twined with grapes and vine leaves, clad in robes of citrine, olive, russet and black. He draws a pentagram in the air before the central door, which transforms into a figure of the Tarot trump of The World, a dancer hanging motionless within a wreath of leaves.

As we pass through we find ourselves in a landscape with a forest upon the left and a cornfield scarlet with poppies on the right. Immediately before us a meadow leads down to a small river with flat stepping stones, upon the other side of which is a limestone cliff that towers upward and from whose summit a waterfall tumbles into a deep pool at its base.

A sound of weeping is heard and we find ourselves approached by a group of mourning women who turn out to be the goddess Demeter and her acolytes, seeking her lost daughter who has been kidnapped by Hades, the Lord of the Underworld. As they pass on we approach the river and cross by the stepping stones. Upon the other side at the foot of the waterfall is an ancient yew tree, half concealing a cave entrance into which we go.

It is cold and damp and dimly lit by a small lamp at the back, and a voice speaks from the darkness asking our reason for entering. It is the dark robed figure of the goddess Hecate, who upon being told of our mission to find Persephone's kingdom indicates a narrow tunnel at the back of the cave and tells us it leads to Hades and we can take it if we dare. She gives us the lamp, however, to help us on our way, and two silver coins.

The tunnel, which leads ever downwards, is dark, cold, damp and slippery, sometimes very low and sometimes very narrow, along a tortuous route through which the wind keeps up a moaning sound like a woman in pain, until we eventually arrive at a vast under-earth cavern. Through the middle runs a dark, swift, deep, flowing river – the Styx – its waters forming a natural barrier between life and death.

A boat is tied to the bank, and by it stands a tall, broad, heavily bearded figure clad only in leather kilt and broad belt with leather pouch, and sandals. It is Charon, the ferryman, and around him shadowy figures throng, bending and swaying as if pleading with him. He strides through the misty throng, makes them draw back, and ushers us into his boat, which he pushes out into the river. Having reached the other side we alight and give him one of our silver coins. He points towards great double gates in the darkness, in the middle of each one is the Hebrew letter Tau. The gates swing open and we pass into a great hall hung with sombre tapestries, at one end of which there sits Hades, the Lord of the Underworld, and at the other a veiled woman wearing a crown beneath her veil and carrying a silver reaping hook.

As we come before Hades, a black hound rises from between his feet, with three heads, and growling. It is the dog Cerberus, who guards his dark master. Somewhat apprehensively we look toward the king, a man of great height and majestic bearing, with hair, eyes and beard as black as night, and a crown of jet.

But as he leans forward we detect a gleam of laughter in his eyes. And his Greek costume reveals the body of a young athlete, not an old man. He stands and leads us towards his consort at the other end of the chamber, Persephone, the Queen of the Dead. At our approach she raises her veil and we look into the laughing face of a young girl crowned with flowers. And we realise that to this place come all, in their time. For Hades and Persephone are also the Lord and Lady of Rebirth, our planetary parents from whom we receive our earthly bodies.

Hades takes us to stand before a mirror and draws back the tapestry that conceals it. The glass seems liquid and full of movement, and within its depths we may see our real and primal spiritual self, as it was before we took form and as it will be at the end of time.

This is the climax of our journey. When the curtain falls back over the mirror we find we are alone with Cerberus who waits to guide us through another door and onto a seashore beneath a night sky filled with stars. Above us the planet Saturn hangs low in the heavens, like a great jewel between its rings, and the Moon rises from the sea, with its light making a pathway to our feet, and stepping a little way along it we feel as if the sea is solid beneath our feet.

Within the orb of the Moon, resting upon the waters, we can see shadowy figures moving until, stepping from its depths, comes the Moon mother herself, robed in black and silver with crescent horns in her hair, bringing the gift of life. She envelops us in her arms and as she does so we feel the scent of all the earth is in her hair and her kiss breathes immortality into us. Then she moves back from us and returning to the Moon sphere, rises with it into the sky, as we return to the shore.

There we find Cerberus barking and playing and leaping alongside his master along the shore. They escort us back to the hall and up to the cavern where Charon waits. He rises and takes the second of our silver coins and gives us passage back over the Styx, from whence we retrace our steps on the road home. Leaving the cave of Hecate we find the earth full of night sounds and scents, and Demeter and her daughter Persephone walking together in the moonlight, to the sound of their laughter in our ears.

These three samples of modern 'path working' from three modern practitioners indicate something of the variety of symbolism and experience within the accepted formal structure of the Paths. Time was when such practical detail, both as regard to symbolism or method, was regarded as highly secret and confined within occult lodges. Fortunately, with the externalisation of the Mysteries that has occurred over the past few decades, these examples have been openly published in the public domain.

This, however, places another challenge, another point of opportunity before us, for the technique now having been revealed, it is up to esoteric students of the twenty-first century not to follow slavishly the approach of any one particular practitioner, but having been appraised of the method and a basic structure of symbolism that is known to work, to undertake their own journeying, following the beaten track that has been laid down by the pioneers of the western esoteric tradition, but allowing themselves freedom of imagination by allowing the images to rise.

FANTASY, BELIEF AND REALITY

"Well, now that we have seen each other," said the Unicorn, "if you'll believe in me, I'll believe in you. Is that a bargain?"

"Yes, if you like," said Alice.

I felt this quotation, from *Through the Looking Glass* by Lewis Carroll, sufficiently important to be displayed prominently at the beginning of *Experience of the Inner Worlds*, a book that I used to teach most of my senior students. Indeed I wrote the book as a result of trying to sort out in my own mind the relationship between occult fantasy, religious belief, and inner plane reality.

The word fantasy should not be taken in a pejorative sense. I use it in the sense of the old adage of the Mysteries that W.E. Butler was fond of quoting: "Fantasy is the ass which carries the Ark." The Ark referred to is, of course, the Ark of the Covenant, containing the Holy of Holies, the Shekinah, God With Us, for the ancient Israelites as they wandered through the wilderness.

That whole story itself, of the twelve tribes being saved from bondage in Egypt, accompanied by miraculous aid and divine guidance, is itself a fantasy. Which is not to say that it is not true – for it holds sufficient truth at various levels to have provided inspiration for at least three world religions, Judah, Christianity and Islam – the 'peoples of the Book', sometimes with rather alarming and unexpected consequences. It has also provided hope and inspiration for various oppressed races as expressed in the spiritual song Swing Low, Sweet Chariot, wherein the singers look to find their way "over Jordan into camp ground" – into freedom.

At a more general level the story is a universal one to be found in various forms in folklore and fairy tale. Its structure is perhaps most simply illustrated in Cinderella, wherein a downtrodden misunderstood heroine, deprived of her birthright, against all odds and the machinations of the wicked and powerful, wins through to marry the handsome prince. It is a paean of human hope, both physical and metaphysical.

One reason advanced for the vogue for Harry Potter is that his situation is based upon the Cinderella formula. So of course is most popular romantic fiction, although the phenomenal success of Harry Potter and his magical powers may perhaps also be a reaction against a generation or so of educational theory that has tried to inflict 'realism' and 'social context' upon children's stories as opposed to traditional fantasy.

However, in the magic of the fairy story, or of miracles in the context of religious belief, there is an expression of faith in a realm of reality that transcends the limitations of the physical world. And in our view, intuitive flights of the imagination are not necessarily a symptom of softening of the brain.

The sceptic may choose to deny that such greater reality exists, that it is all a mirage, projected by our own repressed fears and desires, a form of whistling in the dark. But by rejecting the ladder of faith, the sceptic only proves that he is incapable of mounting higher – which might well be expected if he has dispensed with the means of doing so in the first place! It may seem a pinnacle of achievement in clear-sighted down to earth realism for him, but for the rest of us it looks rather like a wilfully blinkered person trying to make the best of wallowing in the Slough of Despond.

So leaving him in command of his narrow conception of reality let us examine some of the aids to ascent to a wider view, which are available to us through various forms of fantasy and belief.

The Pilgrim's Progress of John Bunyan, to whose Slough of Despond we have referred, is a prime example of the use of the imagination in this manner. It tells the story of Christian's successful journey to the Celestial City in the Delectable Mountains, overcoming the poor advice of Mr Worldly Wiseman, the threats of the foul fiend Apollyon, the distractions of Vanity Fair and detention by Giant Despair in Doubting Castle.

This is fairly simple allegory, as compared to the higher flights of the inspired imagination that are enshrined in myth and legend. Nonetheless, it sold 100,000 copies within ten years of its publication in 1678, an incredible number in those days. And for long it has been, next to the Bible, the most widely read book in English, translated into more than seventy languages.

Fantasy literature as a popular genre, however, extending into the realms of legend and folklore and the myths of all nations, often in the form of children's books that adults like to read, is something of a modern phenomenon.

In this respect it will be interesting to see how the enthusiasm for Harry Potter will last in comparison to Tolkien's *The Lord of the Rings*. Both are fundamentally conservative works. Harry Potter seems in the tradition of the good old-fashioned school yarns, such as *Roy of the Rovers* or *Gwen of Greyfriars*, only with magical accoutrements. The saga of Frodo Baggins and his friends is based more directly upon ancient myth and legend, which can be studied at length in *The Silmarillion* and other treasures salvaged from Tolkien's bottom drawer, as I have been at pains to point out in *The Magical World of the Inklings*.

Whilst myth and legend are a sound underpinning for fantasy that serves to expand our minds, they are not necessarily essential. We have only to look to Lewis Carroll, whom we initially quoted.

Like Tolkien, he was an Oxford don, with a seething subconscious mind seeking for creative expression beyond his university discipline – which in his case was mathematics. Apparently a somewhat repressed character, he found relatively innocent creative expression through photography of young girls, and also, to our universal good fortune, in his attempts to entertain some of them by writing assorted poems and stories including *Alice's Adventures in Wonderland* and *Alice Through the Looking Glass*.

It is doubtful if he was a closet Qabalist or that he held any systematic occult beliefs but his works have provided little gems of wisdom suitable for quotation by esoteric teachers from time to time. "What I tell you three times is true," a maxim of the Bellman in *The Hunting of the Snark*, is a particular favourite of mine, for it illustrates the mechanism of belief systems behind most religious sects and esoteric groups.

This is not as cynical as it may sound, for in most areas of life our assumptions are based not on what we have experienced but on what we have been told. Indeed, it is a practical necessity. However what can be surprising is that it can work to the good, even if based upon error.

Professor Ronald Hutton in *The Triumph of the Moon* and other works, has shown how many of the beliefs of the thriving neo-pagan movement are based not upon prehistoric religious customs but on nineteenth century romantic speculations. However, whatever the truth of his academic assertions, the actual movement seems none the worse for them!

Much the same situation is to be found in the mainstreams of religious belief. Modern biblical criticism may have played havoc with many fundamentalist assumptions, yet has not necessarily destroyed the basis of faith. Whilst human imagination may have embroidered much upon the actual lives of religious leaders, from Moses through Jesus to Mahomet, this may well have proved an enhancement of truth in metaphysical terms.

A similar principle holds true when we come to experiential magical or mystical contact. And here we arrive at the point of Alice's conversation with the Unicorn. Belief in the reality of the other world, of the other being, is a first essential for fruitful interchange to work.

This applies to all contacts, whether expressed in terms of the Holy Spirit, the Communion of Saints, a Spirit Guide or one of the Masters of the Wisdom.

This can of course be the start of a slippery slope to delusion if intelligent belief gives place to blind credulity. The consequences can be disastrous when certain religious sects fall under the sway of self-deluded or criminally manipulating leaders. This can range from fleecing individuals or congregations of their money and possessions to incitement to mass suicide.

For it is not easy to distinguish the true from the false, even in relation to one's own contacts. In my experience the most reliable leaders have privately and sincerely questioned the validity of their contacts from time to time. Certainly this was the case with Dion Fortune, as she reveals in *Spiritualism & Occultism*, on her motives for seeking a consultation with another medium, "that a check-up might be made on my own psychism, for … fear that I may be deluding myself and others owing to subconscious contents getting mixed with my psychism."

This was also the case with her successor Margaret Lumley Brown, who once confided to me that she found it reassuring that the material she got through was taken seriously by sensible down to earth people like me. As a young RAF sergeant, newly admitted into the Fraternity and somewhat awed at a chance meeting with the Arch-Pythoness, I found this candid statement somewhat disconcerting at the time. However, in later years I have come to admire her frankness and to see her point, for it stands to reason that any material coming through one's own consciousness, be it in full old-fashioned trance or modern intuitive channelling, has got to be suspected of a greater or lesser subjective origin. The matter comes down perhaps to terms of percentages, and Alice Bailey has the Tibetan master estimating that only two percent of alleged communication with the Masters is the genuine thing.

However, even subjective material can have its value. As, for example, the realisations of personal meditation, which may be none the worse for being the fruit of one's own higher consciousness.

Something of the subtlety of the matter of fantasy, belief and reality, was adroitly exploited by James Branch Cabell (1879-1958), a writer of fantasy who attracted the admiration of Dion Fortune and Aleister Crowley as well as a number of respected literary figures.

He has somewhat dropped out of sight nowadays although he retains a small discerning following. Over a long literary career starting with historical short stories from about 1902, he came to prominence with a clutch of fantasy novels between 1917 and 1927, commonly conceded to be his best work, and later continued as an erudite and amusing essayist in a more conventional vein until 1955.

Of those fantasy novels, his first, *The Cream of the Jest*, is perhaps the most educative for the way it plays with the issues of fantasy, belief and reality. It is the story of an author, Felix Kennaston, who finds a magical talisman in his garden, which can transport him into another world. There he leads another life, as the character Horvendile, a medieval clerk of no great importance, who at the same time is the creator of the situations in which he finds himself.

In these otherworldly adventures he is in constant pursuit of Ettarre, a young woman of perfect beauty, his picture of the ideal feminine. She is, however, unattainable to him. If ever Horvendile should touch her, even by accident, she and the scene disappears.

It is this unattainability of Ettarre that constitutes in some degree her overwhelming attraction. In comparison to her, women in the real world appear tame, all too human, even if they should prove to be the most pleasant of comrades or most helpful of wives. A great deal of the book alternates scenes of Kennaston's everyday life in Richmond, Virginia, and his adventures in romantic otherworlds as Horvendile.

In this vision of the perfect lover there is a resonance with another writer of metaphysical fiction, Charles Williams, whose assertion is that when we are in love, for that time at least the ideal appears to synchronise with the physical reality. During that time, Williams believes, we are seeing the beloved as he or she really is as an unfallen divine spirit, or as eternally perceived by God.

Cabell's vision is somewhat less theologically elevated. He is more concerned with coming to terms with the physical reality of the everyday human condition after first love has passed, the orange blossom faded, and the confetti swept away. He suggests that the ideal Ettarre is composed of fragments of memory of Kenneston's wife and all the girls he has courted or kissed in the springtime of his life. She is therefore a phantom creature, real enough in fantasy, but untouchable, whose reality depends ultimately upon original physical experience in the real world.

However, what value are we to place upon either experience? Which really is the real world? Or are they as real as each other, but after another manner?

This conundrum is rather neatly put in the circumstances of the story when Kennaston, after flirting with various occult theories, discovers that the magical sigil is in fact not an ancient talisman at all, but the lid of a pot of face cream with a fake antique design on it.

This brings us back to our question of belief, fantasy and reality. The lid of the pot of face cream acted as a doorway to other worlds when he believed in it as a magical talisman. It was he himself who had invested it with the magic by his desire and his belief.

But was it all then a worthless illusion? Not at all, for his experience in the fantasy world brings him to a realisation of the wonder and vibrancy of experience as a whole. He begins to appreciate each moment in the physical world, and sees odd flashes of Ettarre still discernible in his wife. But at the same time this appreciation of vibrant life and experience is also present during his 'dream world' adventures. Ideal and reality reflect upon each other like parallel mirrors.

It might be said that we have an analogy here for the physical and the inner worlds of the occultist. For Cabell does not leave us with a cut and dried answer along the lines that Kennaston hypnotised himself with a fragment of metal and fooled himself into taking his dreams for another reality. The narrator of the story happens to be a knowledgeable occultist, who suggests that those whom he calls the 'Wardens of Earth' have indeed opened windows onto other worlds for Kennaston, by these means.

That is to say, that the sigil, first seen by him on the breast of Ettarre in his first dream vision of her, did actually manifest physically for him to use, but in a completely mundane and explicable way by means of induced expectation combined with coincidence. Thus there is a cosmic law, he suggests, that a doubt must always be left as to the objective existence of other worlds and the means to contact them. Hence the perfectly naturalistic explanation that is possible in this case.

Dion Fortune made no bones about taking the occult theory for granted. And in her work with Maiya Tranchell-Hayes in 1940-2 made notes about the building of what she calls a "Horvendile body" – which is plainly what she regards as a form of astral projection similar to that taught in the knowledge papers of the Golden Dawn.

However, it could be said that this is a somewhat simplistic view of Cabell's intentions, for although Horvendile might well be regarded as an imaginal figure astrally projected, in another sense he could be regarded as just as important, if not more so, than the personality of Kennaston in the physical world, whom he profoundly affects. If this is the case then he comes close to being what is called in esoteric literature the Essential Self.

There are even deeper issues involved than this. One of Horvendile's problems as creator of the worlds which he inhabits is that he has not invested his characters with the ability to recognise who he really is. As far as they are concerned he is a rather deluded minor clerk of little consequence and some rather strange ideas as to his own importance. There is an ironic parallel here, of course, with how Pontius Pilate and members of the Jewish Sanhedrin regarded Jesus.

This is but one more element in Cabell's multifaceted story lines and one of the reasons why he has been taken seriously by a number of literary figures, despite his current neglect.

Aleister Crowley was another occultist who, like Dion Fortune, was impressed by the works of James Branch Cabell, and also possibly for the wrong reasons. No doubt assuming him to be a fellow occultist, Crowley sent him some of his own books to read, and wrote a long appreciative article about Cabell in a literary journal, the July 1923 issue of *The Reviewer* of Richmond, Virginia. Although not renowned for giving undue praise to others Crowley remarkably compares him to Homer and Balzac, no less.

This is no doubt to rate him too highly in the literary pantheon but Cabell does impress through his encyclopaedic knowledge of myths and legends and romantic historical periods. Other serious critics have compared him to heavyweight transcendentalists such as Nathaniel Hawthorne and Herman Melville, which is perhaps nearer the mark.

Crowley was also probably jumping to false conclusions in assuming Cabell to be an occultist, even if he showed knowledge of certain areas of the subject. I have made the same mistake myself with regard to C.S. Lewis, who on the internal evidence of some of his works shows considerable occult knowledge, but who in fact went in some fear and dislike of the subject and largely picked up fragments of knowledge about it from his friends Charles Williams and Owen Barfield. For further evidence of this please refer to my *The Magical World of the Inklings*.

Cabell is in truth somewhat disconcerting as a fantasy writer. His use of irony and wit can often pull us up short just as we thought we had begun to settle down and think we had found our way in the secondary world that, in common with other good fantasy writers, he convincingly provides.

In a typical example in one of the early books of his saga, *Figures of Earth*, Manuel, the hero, a lowly swineherd, is given a magical sword, and sets off on what he has been led to believe is his destined mission to save a beautiful princess from an evil sorcerer. He succeeds in this task, only to find that the sword had been provided to him by the sorcerer himself, who is only too happy to be saved from the nagging tongue of the princess whom he had unfortunately abducted. Manuel takes the hint and refuses to marry the princess himself, preferring a rather plain and down to earth companion.

James Branch Cabell's ambivalent treatment of the clichés of romantic storylines may have come as a result of his own experience as a child, brought up within living memory of the American Civil War in Richmond, Virginia, which had been the capital of the Confederate states. In the social circle of his parents, General Robert E. Lee and his fellow officers were often hailed in terms of a latter day King Arthur and his Knights of the Round Table. At the same time, the war had been lost, and he was privy to conversations in which the all too human failings of these gentlemen were candidly discussed in terms of scandalous and malicious gossip. Thus he had to come to terms with a dual vision of Richmond as a glorious vision of a new Camelot, along with its increasing industrialisation and unglamorous growth as a modern early twentieth century city of the United States of America.

This highly original treatment of the traditional conventions of high fantasy and fairy story may come as something of a shock to us if we seek a good long wallow in a warm bath of romantic adventure. Indeed it is a challenge that has prevented Cabell from becoming as popular a writer as Tolkien or other purveyors of high fantasy. It has latterly encouraged some students of literary criticism to write papers on his role as an early 'post-modernist' and 'subversive fantasist' but such exchanges of academic erudition need not concern us too much.

We do better to turn to his own reflections upon the aims of his writing. These appear principally in two books of essays, *Beyond Life*, written before his series of fantasy books, and *Straws & Prayer Books*, immediately after it. Here, amongst other reflections, he goes so far as to regard romance, or the impulse to idealism, almost in terms of a demiurge, a divine force that prods and inspires us with a certain discontent with things as they are. Through this incurable idealism, that seems not to be shared by other members of the animal kingdom, or even by a fair proportion of the human race, we are urged to seek to improve or embellish the world in which we find ourselves – albeit sometimes in foolish ways.

Ultimately, greater and more permanent questions are asked of us by Cabell. In the starkest philosophical terms he is asking "What is the reality of reality?" Without becoming involved in weighty philosophical debate where we may soon be out of our intellectual depth, there are nonetheless simpler and more answerable questions that derive from this. In pragmatic terms, as occultists, what are we expecting of the alternative world we call the 'inner planes'? What is its relation to conditions in the physical world? Is either more important, the outer world or the inner world? How do they relate, one to another?

The study of fantasy literature is one of the more diverting ways of undertaking such a task, and of this literature, which used to be well represented in the library of the Society of the Inner Light, there are many kinds. It ranges from Tolkien's *The Lord of the Rings*, which was the subject of an Inner Light study group within months of its first appearing. It passes through various mind stretching annals of science fiction, which can provide an imaginative introduction to wider metaphysical views than even *The Cosmic Doctrine*. And eventually it can pass on to darker, profound metaphysical classics such as David Lindsay's *Voyage to Arcturus* which C.S. Lewis even considered to be of demonic inspiration. Nor should we ignore such recent phenomena as the Discworld of Terry Pratchett which presents some esoteric truths in a humorous spirit. Much of this may be a far cry from, and rather more demanding than the adventures of Harry Potter, but nonetheless all may well be ways that the 'Wardens of Earth' have chosen to teach certain elements of the secret wisdom to a modern secular public. As committed students to this same secret wisdom, we do not do well to miss out on all of this!

CHRETIEN DE TROYES – THE FIRST ARTHURIAN ROMANCER

ESOTERIC RESEARCH into the Arthurian legends is like a great archaeological dig down through many strata. Strata that are, moreover, often disturbed from their original neat layers. Most English readers rely upon the works of Sir Thomas Malory, the obscure knight and possible horse thief from the time of the Wars of the Roses, who spent his time in prison translating old French prose romances from two hundred and fifty years before his time. His work is one of the flowers of English literature, one of the first to come from Caxton's printing press of 1485.

In latter years some of his French sources have also been translated into handy paperback editions including *The Death of King Arthur, The Quest of the Holy Grail* as Penguin Classics, and in Oxford World's Classics *Lancelot of the Lake*. All done with scholarly accuracy although nothing like Malory's great style. They are culled from an immense prose work in Old French that was the work of several hands in the earlier years of the 13th century, in what was the medieval equivalent of a modern soap opera. Various authors contributed their bit to a complex tapestry of evolving tales concerning various ladies, knights, enchanters and faeries.

However the first tales of King Arthur's court to come down to us date from some fifty years before these works, in the narrative poems of Chrétien de Troyes, who worked in the court of the Count of Champagne and later that of the Count of Flanders. These too are available in English translation in the Everyman series as *Arthurian Romances* (although excluding the unfinished *Story of the Graal*).

The five Arthurian romances that come down to us from Chrétien's pen concern the knights Erec (or Geraint), Cligés, Lancelot, Yvain and Perceval – although other knights such as Gawain and of course King Arthur and Queen Guenevere also appear in them. Some of these stories also appear in a collection of Welsh stories, translated and published as *The Mabinogion*. Whether they pre-date or post-date those of Chrétien is a matter of some debate. Did they copy from Chrétien or did Chrétien copy from them? A middle way suggests that they borrowed from a common source.

Whatever the truth of the matter, it is fairly safe to say that all stem from a common tradition. That tradition being of considerable antiquity and largely oral, and having its roots in the western parts of the British Isles and the continental seaboard, that is to say, Ireland, Wales, the Cornish peninsula and Brittany.

Chrétien, the courtly romancer, was adroit in latching on to this Arthurian tradition as a source for his narrative poems, and in European literary terms he was first in the field – apart from the fragmentary mentions of the Arthurian tradition in Geoffrey of Monmouth's Latin *History of the Kings of Britain* and its free translations into Norman French by Wace (who introduced the Table Round) and Middle English by Layamon (who introduced the elves at Arthur's birth and departure for Avalon).

What is particularly fascinating about Chrétien's work is that we can see him struggling between the courtly conventions and expectations of his day and the ancient material which held a perennial fascination for his listeners but which no-one could really understand. Thus fragments of folklore and legend appear as a picturesque background, complete with occasional supernatural wonders, whilst the heroes and heroines of his stories think and behave entirely according to the assumptions of aristocratic society in 12th century France.

We therefore have the intriguing task, in reading Chrétien's Arthurian romances, of trying to pick the meat of ancient tradition from the bones of 12th century fashionable conventions, although it must be said that the latter too have their own great interest and charm. Chrétien is also a great literary stylist, although octosyllabic couplets in the Champagnois dialect of Old French require a certain dedication to appreciate, and modern editions of his work in France now usually carry a translation into modern French.

Chrétien's origins are obscure but he seems to have been educated by the church (as were most in those days), and to have served his apprenticeship in translations of classical Latin texts, principally from Virgil and Ovid. However, he came into his own when he latched onto the Arthurian fashion.

His first, *Erec and Enid*, (whose equivalent is *Geraint and Enid* in *The Mabinogion*), concerns the story of a knight who after displaying great heroics settles down with his lady Enid and neglects the life of valour. Stung into action by taunts of the court he goes off on a quest, with Enid in tow, proving his manhood and knightly prowess in no uncertain fashion. Poor Enid has a lot to put up with in all of this, and his macho display is even more crudely portrayed in the version in the Welsh. However, what is of interest to the esoteric researcher is not a moral story about a conflict between married life and one of adventure (a theme which is still to be found in Wild West films today) but the nature of some of the adventures in which he finds himself.

One of these is the Joy of the Court, which is obviously a sequence of some kind of redemptive initiation of a society by a charismatic hero, who enters some kind of sacred space to do battle with a guardian for a maiden and a hawk. And in the background of the whole story is a theme of the Principle of Sovereignty, as part of his duty is to avenge an insult to Queen Guenevere from an evil knight, proud woman and a dwarf, that she has suffered whilst wandering in the woods. This is a throwback to ancient themes of the kidnapping of the Spring Maiden by the Lord of the Underworld. Later he also has considerable assistance from one of the 'little people' who is obviously a thinly disguised king of an inner plane kingdom. All these supernatural beings and forces are however rendered into contemporary human characters by Chrétien.

His next romance goes off at something of a tangent, no doubt influenced by contemporary interest in Byzantium, tales of whose magnificence were filtering back at this time by those returning from the crusades. Cligés is a Byzantine knight who goes to Logres seeking membership of King Arthur's Fellowship of the Table Round, thus getting the best of both worlds. His father Alexander had done much the same thing, and had married Gawain's sister before returning to Byzantium. Cligés, their son, thus follows in his footsteps, and distinguishing himself in jousts against the best knights of the Table Round, Sagramore, Lancelot, Perceval and Gawain.

The story is a strange concoction that has been described as having an 'anti-Tristram' motivation, for Chrétien has been considered something of a middle class moralist who did not greatly approve of the popular tale of Tristram and Iseult who had been adulterously attracted to each other and who showed great ingenuity in betraying her husband King Mark. In his story of Cligés and Fénice, Chrétien has his couple avoid adultery by an astute application of drugs. Her husband is doped into thinking he is enjoying his wife's favours when all the time the experience is only in his mind, as she lies chastely beside him. Then Fénice escapes from her loveless marriage to her lover's arms by taking a drug herself that makes it appear that she has died. Once respectably deceased as far as the world is concerned, she then is recovered from the sepulchre and resuscitated, to enjoy a loving relationship with Cligés at last.

Ridiculous as all this may seem, the theme of entering the tomb and then joining a lover in a subterranean love nest, adjoined to a secret garden in which they lie naked under a central tree has resonances with myths such as Orpheus and Eurydice, not to say Adam and Eve. This is a stratum of ancient lore that goes far beyond 12th century courtly fictions on how best to manage loveless marriages and illicit lovers – both of which were rife, in fantasy if not in fact, owing to the social conventions of the time. Women who inherited land or were connected to powerful families were married off for dynastic reasons, not infrequently as children.

In Chrétien's third romance, *The Knight of the Cart*, we follow the adventures of Lancelot, who figures as a paradigm for the faithful

Chrétien de Troyes – The First Arthurian Romancer

and devoted lover according to the conventions conceived by the Courts of Love at Poitiers. These Courts flourished particularly from 1168 to 1174 when Eleanor of Aquitaine renewed the ducal court to its former glories as a centre of Troubadour minstrelsy. She was assisted in this by her eldest daughter Marie, Countess of Champagne, under whose patronage Chrétien flourished at the court at Troyes.

It would seem however that Marie leaned rather heavily upon Chrétien to produce a story to accord with her romantic inclinations and theories. The lovesick Lancelot undergoes all kinds of humiliations to prove his devotion to Queen Guenevere, culminating at a tournament where he alternately fights as well as he can and the worst that he can at Guenevere's command. Chrétien eventually abandoned the tale, and handed it over to a fellow poet to finish, which suggests that he may have rebelled against this petticoat editing. Nonetheless there are more than a few traces of ancient material being used.

The queen, in this story, is actually abducted and taken off to a country from whence no-one ever returns, which suggests an underworld country, or possibly one beyond the grave. She is however rescued by Lancelot who goes on a lengthy and arduous quest to find her. This begins with him fighting a powerful knight at a ford (a passage between two worlds), and eventually making his way to the heart of the forbidden country and to the queen's side. This involves an arduous crossing of a sword bridge over a raging torrent that is likened to the rivers of hell.

Once within reach of the queen there follows an actual physical consummation of their secret love, which, in terms of the conventions of courtly love is the final one of seven stages of courtship – euphemistically known as the 'giving of thanks' to the lover for his devotion.

Whether it was Chrétien who began the convention of the secret love between Lancelot and Guenevere that in Malory brings about the fall of the Fellowship of the Table Round is open to question. Dion Fortune has her own theories which she expounded in *The Arthurian Formula* in terms of socio-sexual dynamics, although another speculation could concern the faery connections of both these characters. Lancelot du Lac was raised by the Lady of the Lake from infancy to knighthood in an underwater faery kingdom, whilst Guenevere herself may well have had faery origins.

Her very name means 'the white lady', which is the traditional faery colour. She was the daughter of the evocatively named King Leodegranz (the great lion), who presented her with the Round Table as a dowry when she married Arthur. In its wider analysis the Round Table is the circle of the zodiacal stars, and in ancient time Leo and its star Regulus was the start of that starry belt through which the sun and planets proceed. Arthur himself, as being the destined king of it, is of course associated with the polar axis of the spinning Earth, one name for the northern constellation of the Great Bear being Arthur's Wain. From this could be spun the theory that Guenevere and Lancelot and even Arthur are star beings to a greater or lesser degree.

Indeed this is not far removed from some of the mythopeoic racial memories evoked by Tolkien in his tales about the elves – who appear tangentially in the celebrated *The Lord of the Rings*. However, their origin and racial history is treated in greater systematic detail in *The Silmarillion* in which many esoteric and religious traditions are preserved and given new life, from Atlantis (Tolkien's Númenor) to the fall of angels, elves and humankind. It may seem a far cry from Tolkien to Chrétien de Troyes but nonetheless through their common mythopeoic concerns the linkages are there.

In his fourth romance Chrétien seems to have shaken off the influence of Countess Marie of Champagne, and in *Yvain*, or the *Knight of the Lion*, we have lots of quite overt ancient faery material, although treated in quite a matter of fact manner. Yvain commences his quest by meeting a lady at a fountain, directed there by an incredibly ugly and monstrous Lord of the Animals. Once there he evokes her inner guardian by blowing a horn which brings about a great storm followed by a gentle peace with the singing of birds in all the trees. After vanquishing her guardian he is constrained more or less to take his place. This immediate marrying of his victim's widow may seem bizarre in sociological terms but carries the truth of ancient myths of the hero.

There is in Chrétien still the usual 12th century courtly concerns about right aristocratic behaviour. Yvain's, in this sense, is an opposite counterpart to Erec's. Whereas Erec fell short at first by putting too much emphasis on courtly life as opposed to the life of action, Yvain falls short by neglecting his wife and spending too much time on adventures. In the end he realises the error of his ways and puts things to rights, but the importance of the story for us lies in its incidental supernatural elements. These include him being cured from madness by a potion from Morgan le Fay, and his protection by a lion after he had rescued it from a serpent. This provides the alternative title for the romance, and much scholarly ink has flowed in trying to interpret the significance of this beast, the most prosaic and unimaginative being that it stems from a rehash of the Roman story of Androcles and the Lion.

Chrétien's final romance is the one for which he is perhaps most remembered, although he never finished it, not even deputing some other hand to complete it. It has since been completed in various ways by a number of independent 'continuators' a generation and more after Chrétien laid down his pen. Each has been eager to put his own interpretation upon the Graal – and the Cistercian monks have perhaps been most responsible for its configuration as a chalice, or even the cup used by Jesus at the Last Supper or used to catch the blood of the crucified Christ by Joseph of Arimathea.

It became a courtly convention of Chrétien not to announce the name of the hero of his romances until very well on into the tale. To aid and abet this guessing game he entitled them somewhat cryptically. Thus what we more often call *Lancelot* was *The Knight of the Cart*, and what we call *Yvain* was *The Knight of the Lion*, and the tale about Perceval, the innocent fool who became a knight, he called *The Knight of the Graal* – which is to say *The Knight of the Plate*. All titles perhaps designed to titillate the curiosity of a medieval audience.

In Old French, 'graal' is not a common word, but where it has been used it refers to a large serving dish – of a size suitable for carrying a decent sized salmon.

Whether we have a line here onto the pagan Celtic salmon of wisdom on the one hand, and ichthus the early symbol for the Christ on the other, is open to conjecture. It can join the various images that many since have put forward, from the Cauldron of Ceridwen to the Cup of the Last Supper.

By the time Chrétien wrote this romance he seems to have left the employ of Countess Marie of Champagne. Upon the death of her husband, Henry the Liberal, she had gone into deep mourning and taken to the religious life. It would appear that Chrétien moved on to employment with the neighbouring and highly influential Philip Count of Flanders. Indeed he specifically says at the start of his romance that the tale comes from a book provided to him by the Count.

Scholars tend to dismiss this claim, simply on the grounds, it seems, that no such manuscript has ever turned up. Although that seems hardly surprising, for there are countless medieval manuscripts that have not survived until modern times.

Internal evidence suggests that there is material in the original tale that stems from some Middle Eastern metaphysical sect. One of Chrétien's successors, Wolfram von Eschenbach, goes so far as to claim that Chrétien got the story all wrong and that he alone has the authentic version. This, it might be said, is par for the course in any esoteric tradition. Wolfram's version has appealed particularly to the Germanic imagination so that it forms the basis for Wagner's operatic cycle.

If Chrétien was indeed vouchsafed a manuscript by Philip of Flanders, running true to form he is likely to have adapted it somewhat to his own way of thought. Most scholars assume that he died before he could finish it, but there may be other reasons for its unfinished state, no-one can say. However the history of the family of Philip of Flanders suggests that some kind of metaphysical manuscript might well have been brought back from the Middle East. For Philip himself and his father Thierry and his father before him had all been constant pilgrims to the Holy Land, even before the start of the crusades. His mother, indeed, was so enamoured of the Kingdom of Jerusalem that she settled in a nunnery there, whilst he himself met his death there in 1191 at the seige of Acre. Did, one wonders, Chrétien perhaps accompany him there? And if so, what became of him?

What we care to read into the tale as left by Chrétien about the adventures of the Innocent Fool, the Son of the Widow, who failed to ask the Graal Question in order to save the Waste Land from its overlying curse, is up to us. Many have put their own interpretation upon the Graal, the Graal Maiden, and the Maimed and the Fisher King. To the student of history there are also interesting resonances with the state of the Frankish kingdom of Jerusalem in those times. It was indeed for a period ruled by a maimed king, the saintly but tragic Baldwin the Leper. At the same time the kingdom was riven by internal political strife, and wasted away by its own internal corruption, much as did the body of its boy king from his crippling disease.

But all that is another story. Yet the history of those times contains elements that invite comparison even with the stuff of Arthurian romance. Charismatic characters abound, including those who claimed a faery connection. Richard Coeur de Lion, who led the 3rd Crusade, proudly boasted of being of 'the Devil's Brood' on account of his descent from Fulke the Black of Anjou who allegedly married a water sprite. The Lusignan family, whose family fortress was in Richard's ducal domain, claimed descent from Melusine, with other faery links to Brittany and the ancient Scottish kingdom of Albany. By strange tricks of fortune they became kings of Jerusalem and Cyprus, founding a dynasty that lasted for three hundred years. The original conqueror of Jerusalem himself, the pious Godfrey of Bouillon, Duke of Lower Lorraine, was accounted a descendent of Lohengrin, the Knight of the Swan in the legends of the Rhine.

This may seem like gross superstition nowadays, or an attempt by those of less than the purest noble blood to upstage their social superiors by transcendental connections. However, even history, at the remove of eight centuries, can take on the lineaments of legend and ancient lore. Therefore it may be no waste of our time to take as much account of these tales as we do of the literary legends, to see what ancient wisdom may be preserved therein.

Thus the four husbands of Isabella of Jerusalem, each having a different human characteristic, may have something to teach us that might have some connection with the four psychological functions of Jung or their esoteric equivalent. Humphrey the Arabic scholar, Conrad the fierce warrior, Henry the urbane courtier, Aimery the adroit adventurer. Or the four charismatic daughters of one of the early kings, Melisende, Alice, Constance and Jovetta, women larger than life, who became mistresses of the three great crusader domains, of Jerusalem, Tripoli and Antioch and of a nunnery at Bethany. There is something to be learned perhaps from a study of the history of 12th century characters themselves from a mythical point of view, as well as the romances and legends that fascinated them and their leading narrative poet, Chrétien de Troyes.

THE ELEMENTAL TIDES

A LONG STANDING tradition within the Fraternity of the Inner Light has been an awareness of the flow of Elemental Tides throughout the year. If we are aware of how these tides flow, and consciously try to work with them, we can find them to be very real aids to spiritual growth, to say nothing of our feeling of wellbeing within the world. The human soul in its voyage through the years is rather in the nature of a small boat. If we want to make real or comfortable progress it helps to be aware of the prevailing winds and tides.

The nature of the Tides, as used for many years by Dion Fortune, her inner teachers, and therefore her students, has been:

From Vernal Equinox to Summer Solstice – the **Fire Tide**
From Summer Solstice to Autumnal Equinox – the **Earth Tide**
From Autumnal Equinox to Winter Solstice – the **Air Tide**
From Winter Solstice to Vernal Equinox – the **Water Tide**

This is not the only way of taking account of the many inner tides and currents that swirl about us. Dane Rudhyar, for example, in his book *The Pulse of Life*, analyses the passage of the year with an emphasis upon the zodiacal signs. Another way is related to the phases of the Moon. Or of course there are other astrological cycles concerned with the movement of the planets, such as the thirty year one related to Saturn, which is more or less the time it takes to move throughout anyone's horoscope to get back to where it started – a cycle which takes the Moon only twenty eight days. In *The Cosmic Doctrine* the passage of major comets is commented upon, which of course have a cycle of their own – the famous Halley's Comet for example appearing about every 78 years. Other astronomical phenomena include the recent sight of Venus transiting the face of the Sun in something like a 120 year cycle, so that no-one is likely to experience such occasions twice or even to live through a single cycle whilst in the flesh, whatever they might portend.

Leaving aside these various astrological options, all of which have their validity at one level or another, the system we treat of here is in terms of a much more simple and direct awareness of Elemental and Human interaction, of life on Earth, at any rate for those who live in a temperate climate in the northern hemisphere.

It is based on the principle of the four qualities of human consciousness and their particular relevance at various times of the year. Thus the initiatives of new burgeoning life in the Springtime are of the Spirit (the equivalent of Fire); the Summer time calls for a celebration of the well being of the Body (the equivalent of Earth) not least because it is a time for holidays; the Autumn is a time of review, and of the Mind (the equivalent of Air), focussing on what has been achieved in the immediate past along with aspirations for the future, a time which sees much enrolment in educational and vocational courses; whilst the rigours of the Winter season, hard enough even in our cosseted times, bring reactions of the Emotions (the equivalent of Water).

The rather mundane examples we have cited as to their application have a greater depth the more we link them to their correspondence with the Elemental powers. Indeed the more we realise this connection, the greater will the effect upon us be, hence they are particularly relevant to the lives of initiates and esoteric students who are consciously striving to work with the inner forces of life in a practical way.

The four seasons correspond to major points of the solar year of course. The Spring and Autumnal equinoxes mark the point where the Sun is directly over the Equator, and thus day and night are equally divided there. The Summer solstice is when the Sun appears to be at its most northern latitude, to bring us the longest day and shortest night; whilst the Winter solstice is when it appears

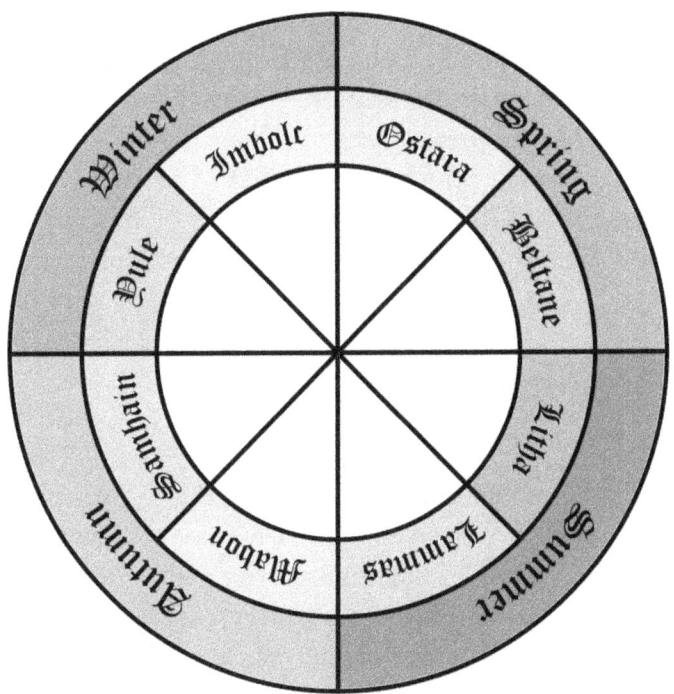

to be at its most southern latitude, bringing us in the northern hemisphere the shortest day and the longest night. This variation is caused by the tilt of the Earth's axis relevant to its orbit round the Sun, as despite appearances, it is the movement of the Earth around the Sun that determines these seasons. If the Earth's axis were completely upright rather than tilted, and its orbit completely circular rather than eliptical, there would be no seasons.

Each of the four seasons, or quarter of the year, lasts approximately twelve weeks, but they can helpfully be divided into two periods of six weeks, by recognising a mid-point in each that is often called a Cross Quarter day. These are generally celebrated on or about the first or second day of May, June, November and February. They are not quite so rigidly fixed as the Quarter Days because in origin they are Celtic Fire festivals, calculated not from the solar year but from the lunar year of 13 equal 28-day months. Derivations of them may indeed be celebrated at any time up to the 15th of the month as a result of the change to the Gregorian calendar in 1582 (and considerably later in the northwest of Europe). But we need not bother ourselves too much with astronomical calculations, for in practice a certain degree of latitude seems to have done no harm to their significance or observance. We shall gain all we need by simply being aware of the prevailing tone of each Tide, regarding the various festivals from a mix of traditional Christian or pagan feasts, festivals and holy days, whether solar, lunar or cosmic.

Spring and the Tide of Fire
midpoint May Day or Beltane

Let us start by considering the Fire Tide that commences at the Vernal Equinox. We start with this because to the initiate, as indeed to all members of the human race did they but know it, the Spring Equinox at the beginning of the third week in March is a particularly important point in the year. It is the time when the human spirit seeks to express whatever it has been germinating during the Winter period. The deepest urges and aspirations of the soul, or higher self, seek expression at this time of year in the outer world. The spirit is quickened by a mighty impulse that works through the whole of nature from the loftiest heights.

It is the time of year when, becoming aware of this stirring of the spirit within, we can look up to the angelic spheres above and hear all around and within us the winged body of the spirit soaring in the upper spheres. This is the time when the inner forces of the Earth stir with great strength, drawn forth by the strong cosmic forces of the outer regions; and so it is that these forces of activity pass through our being, bringing the potential for the ecstasy and the joy of creativity on whatever level we are capable of responding.

All Fool's Day on April 1st marks the beginning of the esoteric year, with the significance of the innocent Fool of the Tarot trumps, or Parsifal the Grail hero, going forth in search of experience. It approximates to the moveable feast of Easter (which takes its date from the first full moon after the Vernal Equinox) with particular relevance to the Resurrection on Easter Day followed by the Ascension of Christ into Heaven and the Descent of the Holy Spirit at Whitsun or Pentecost, forty days after Easter. All this is foreshadowed by the very first Christian Festival after the Vernal Equinox, the Annunciation of the Archangel Gabriel to the Virgin Mary on 25th March.

In the midst of the period comes May Day, or the old Celtic festival of Beltain, a feast of Belenos, the Shining One, when the faery doors of the sidhe were reckoned to open, with the inspirational manifestation of the poetic powers of Taliesin and Pryderi. It marked the real beginning of Summer, leaves beginning to show and flowers making the meadows colourful, when herds were let out into the open fields from their winter stockades. It was also the time for new ventures. The May Day festivities saw the erection of the Maypole and dancing round it to decorate it, with the procession of the May Queen, sometimes represented as the Virgin Mary, whose month May is. It is also the time of Flora, the spirit of returning summer. Dancing took place with green branches, and a hobby horse associated with fertility a feature of the dance, along with characters from Robin Hood and the greenwood legends. Garlands would be wound round staves, or placed in wreaths at their tops, very often of cowslips on peeled willow wands. Hoop garlands might have balls tossed through them or brought together to form a globe. Rising early to wash in the May dew was a purifying and healing rite, and silverware might also be paraded.

Those who are capable of rising to the greater spiritual heights need most particularly at this time of year to make contact with the natural forces of the Elements, to work close to nature and the Elemental etheric levels, which can be contacted particularly strongly between May and the Summer Solstice as this great Fire Tide passes on to the great Midsummer festival of the triumph of the warmth and light, and also of the Spirit.

Summer and the Tide of Earth
midpoint Lammas or Lughnasadh, Midsummer Day

In the Christian year the Solstice marks the birth of John the Baptist, the Forerunner, and as a fitting conclusion to the Fire Tide it is also an important fire festival, with bonfires, torch processions and flaming tar barrels or wheels, with blazing gorse carried around the cattle or driving them between two fires, to protect them from harm, and dances involving passing through fire performed. Other customs were the strewing of hay or rushes, mowing meadows, or decorating wells with floral pictures.

The Summer Solstice is a time when the cosmic powers – some of them from remote distances – make especial contact esoterically with the inner Earth as well as with human nature at the commencement of the great Earth Tide. It signifies the consummation of the Solar Power, bringing through a train of cosmic and elemental power of many types which contacts the Earth and can contact us, so as to be grounded and expressed in this great Earth Tide.

The period in July leading up to August and Lammastide can thus be a time of testing and trial for many people who are sensitive, resulting either in psychic unbalance through an uprush from the underworld, or a feeling of physical lethargy as the Sun starts noticeably to descend towards the Autumnal Equinox. The solsticial noon of the year is past. Yet it is a great Earth tide that in the old country year saw the bringing of the first fruits into the church, either as first corn of the year or the new bread made from it. It was in old Celtic mythology the feast of Lugh Longhand, the sun god, celebrated with games and contests, fairs and the celebration of marriages.

In the calendar of Our Lady it brings the great feminine festival of the Assumption of the Blessed Virgin into Heaven, when the unique role of the Virgin Mary is emphasised as first member of the church and exemplar and advocate for the human race. That it is her *physical* assumption into heaven that is mooted, is an important hint to the profound interlinking to be found between heaven and earth, or Kether and Malkuth, and particularly to be contemplated in this Earth Tide. It is of particular significance for the divinisation of natural life, a time for the Planetary Being to be brought into mind. In ancient Egypt it was the time of the inundation of the Nile which brought life to the land, heralded by the rising of the bright star Sirius, the Dog Star, of Anubis, Opener of the Ways.

This is in keeping with the ancient Celtic feast of Lughnasadh, the high summer gathering, the hay harvest in and the corn harvest about to come, a time for arranging marriages and showing off horses with competitive games, and primordially a feast of the goddess of sovereignty. Another day of importance in the Christian year is that of the Transfiguration, on August 6th, when Jesus on the Mount of Illumination appeared to his three senior disciples in a revelation of heavenly and earthly conjunction, a coded vision of past, present and spiritual future yet to come.

Two other of the most Earthy of spiritual Christian realisations are celebrated during this Tide, Corpus Christi on 13th June and the Triumph of the Cross on September 14th. And thus the tide proceeds into the Autumnal Equinox and the time of Harvest Home, marked by a garlanded and loaded hay wain with revellers upon it. Of particular significance was the last sheaf cut, held to hold the spirit of the corn and often made into a corn dolly, sometimes shaped like a pyramid, and kept throughout the ensuing year.

Autumn and the Tide of Air
midpoint Samhain, Halloween, All Saints, All Souls Day

The first Christian feast after the Equinox that marks the phase change from Earth to Air, from outer to inner, is that of St. Michael and all Angels on 29th September, or Michaelmas, with its association of victory after the final ingathering of the harvest. It is a time for bringing former actions and future ideas to mind. A time when not only are individual esoteric positions and functions assessed but the work of the Hierarchy itself is reviewed in its functional relation to the greater whole.

Then at the mid point of the season comes Hallowe'en with All Saints and All Souls, recognising the human as well as angelic inhabitants of the Unseen. In popular belief a time when souls were released from Purgatory for forty eight hours and candles lit for them at windows and a little feast set out for them. A time for remembrance of absent friends and relations, particularly those deceased. In many Christian countries it is still the time when families make journeys of considerable distance to lay flowers upon the graves of their loved ones. In the old agricultural years it was the time when livestock was brought in from the fields, to be stockaded or killed, an opportunity for feasting, similar to the Jewish passover, when blood was marked on lintels as a protection for the coming year, or a small carcase thrown over the roof. The modern celebration of Remembrance Day on November 11th takes the principle to a higher level.

The psychic side of the Tide is shown as the traditional time for trying to read the future by various spells involving candle and mirror. Dressing up as ghosts with illuminated hollow turnips, swedes and pumpkins is a lighter aspect of the forces to be reckoned with. This marked the beginning of winter in the Celtic year, with Samhain under the influence of the Cailleach, the Hag of Winter, for after the plentiful autumn is foreseen the coming of a barren time. It is the time of the death of the hero Cúchulainn.

There is a Christian resonance with this on the 8th December with the Feast of the Immaculate Conception of the Blessed Virgin Mary which also marks the coming of Advent, which includes anticipation of the ending of the world as well as the coming of the Messiah.

Winter and the Tide of Water
midpoint Oimelc, Festival of Lights, Candlemass

The Winter Solstice represents the Midnight Sun and Solar Power communicating with the human spirit and its drawing in and concentration into the heart of each individual, the incarnation of the spirit, spiritual fire coming down and making intimate contact with the Earth.

The spiritual sub-plane of the Earth Mother is contacted at the Winter Solstice. This contact brings through the highest levels from which the Earth first drew her forces. They include the Logoidal powers which operate at Christmas and the great Pan force which operates at the Winter Solstice. The nativity of Mithra as well as of Jesus.

And with the passing of the Winter Solstice comes the great Cleansing or Water Tide. The contact of the Water Tide acts upon the emotional body of each one of us. Its action tends to eliminate all those things which prevent the intensity of the feelings, for the action of water may bring about a much wider, broader, comprehensive range of feeling, so that we may learn in time to feel with a blade of grass, with an angel, or with any of God's creatures. Anything that comes between ourselves and the way of personal destiny or service may be swept away by the Water Tide. And because it brings about a gradual expansion of feeling, a broadening of the range of sympathy, it has tended to become associated with emotional discomfort and pain, hence its former alternative title of the Tide of Destruction. It is in fact more a spring cleaning of the soul for the new life to come in at the Vernal Equinox, when a new cycle of life in the initiate's year can be started.

The half point is Oimelc or Imbolc, loosening of winter's grip, new lambs born, ewes in milk, the Feast of Brigit or St. Bride. A popular game played on a chequered board saw an old witch armed with a dragon and a lion doing battle with a fair maiden armed with a lamb and a hail storm, representatives of the Cailleach or Hag of Winter and Brigit the Spring Maiden, for which reason she was later credited with being foster mother of the Christ child. This time also marks the feast of the Purification of Blessed Virgin Mary or her Presentation at the Temple, which took the place of a very ancient Festival of Isis, when little boats bearing candles were set forth upon the waters.

In the Christian year the close of this Tide coincides with the period of Lent, a time of introspection, spiritual preparation, fasting and repentance. The element of renewal is also marked by the Feast of St Matthias on 24th February, who was the disciple elected to replace Judas amongst the twelve. All these teachings have application within the human soul, within ourselves, and so at this time we look to abandon all in which we have fallen short in the past and to take on the new as we seek to enter upon another new year in the cycle of the Elemental Tides.

As one of the inner plane adepti responsible for this teaching recorded:

"We who are the Adepts of the Elements and know their actions and work with them, hope and strive to bring you all to a greater realisation and awareness of the action of the forces. So that by co-operating with them you can rejoice and be glad, even in the very midst of conflict and pain. It is a very necessary part of the Aquarian plan. It is not enough that you should accept the actions of the various phases, but you should be able to accept them with gladness and not sorrow. There is a very great deal of difference between acceptance with joy that comes of understanding and the ability to get behind the action, and the one who accepts in ignorance and is swept along blindly by the currents of the forces."

DO YOU BELIEVE IN FAIRIES…?

THE 2004-5 pantomime season saw me accompanying my granddaughter to a performance of *Peter Pan* by J. M. Barrie, a classic piece of Edwardian whimsy that saw its first production exactly one hundred years ago, and is still going strong, with its royalties donated by the author to the Great Ormond Street Children's Hospital.

Perhaps the most famous line in the play comes when the fairy Tinkerbell is dying, through having voluntarily consumed some poison destined for Peter Pan by the "blacker than night" villain Captain Hook. As her light fades, so Peter Pan appeals to the audience to save her by affirming their belief in fairies. As a result of the tumultuous response to this appeal to their faith, Tinkerbell miraculously recovers and her light shines forth ever more brightly.

It is perhaps a reflection of our times that on the performance I attended this year, rejigged into the form of a pantomime, this sequence was omitted. Modern children are perhaps assumed to be too sophisticated. It was thus with a slight sense of retrospective satisfaction that I noted that the run had come to a premature end due to lack of support. Perhaps the adapters of the script should have put more faith in the wisdom of tradition and the generous hearts of children.

There are of course many different conceptions of what fairies might be, what they might do, and what they may look like. Our Edwardian predecessors, like the Victorians before them, tended rather to a juvenile prettification of them, all gauze wings and frilly knickers. Indeed they tended to treat even the angels in much the same way – as simpering acolytes in high church dalmatics rather than the awesome powers described in the Biblical visions of fiery serpents and flaming swords, whirling wheels rimmed with eyes, or shimmering lights like hot coals. So is there a similar gap between cute flower fairies of the nursery and the "lordly ones of the hollow hills".

The fairy tradition is an ancient and a universal one. A recently published popular illustrated encyclopaedia of them, *The Great Encyclopaedia of Faeries*, lists close on a hundred different types, which for convenience are divided into Maidens of Clouds and of Time; Faeries of the Hearth; Golden Queens of the Middle World; Faeries of Rivers and the Sea; Maidens of the Green Kingdoms; and Ethereal Ones of Infinite Dreams. A work, as it happened, that originated in France, the translation of which has been supported by the Cultural Service of the French Embassy in London. For some reason, the French have a distinguished record in the recognition of the faery kingdoms and writing intelligently about them.

Not that the English language is wholly lacking in the subject. A classic work is that of a young American student, W.Y. Evans Wentz whose doctoral thesis for the University of Rennes, in Brittany, was published in 1911 as *The Fairy-Faith in Celtic Countries*. It is a record of field work in Ireland, Scotland, Wales, Brittany, Cornwall and the Isle of Man, and the text is an important milestone in being one remove away from the older anthropological orthodoxy of J.G. Frazer and *The Golden Bough*, that assumed that mythopoeic wisdom was simply misapplied logic by ignorant savages attempting to explain natural phenomena.

However, Evans Wentz, writing at a time when Sigmund Freud was beginning to make waves in the intellectual world, did incline toward a psychological explanation for the phenomena reported in his field work. This approach, it should be said, is still quite fashionable, particularly in light of the broader interpretations of the Jungian school, although there are many of us nowadays, as of old, who incline to belief in a more objective metaphysical reality.

Nonetheless Evans Wentz was sufficiently impressed by intelligent seers of his time to give attention to the possibility of taking evidence at face value, and his book is indeed dedicated to the contemporary Irish mystics W. B. Yeats and 'A.E.' It is worth quoting his dedication in full for those who are prepared to read between the lines:

> This Book depends chiefly upon the oral and written testimony so freely contributed by its many Celtic authors – the peasant and the scholar, the priest and the scientist, the poet and the business man, the seer and the non-seer – and in honour of them I dedicate it to two of their brethren in Ireland: A.E., whose unwavering loyalty to the fairy-faith has inspired much that I have herein written, whose friendly guidance in my study of Irish mysticism I most gratefully acknowledge; and William Butler Yeats, who brought to me at my own alma mater in California the first message from Fairyland, and who afterwards in his own country led me through the haunts of Fairy Kings and Queens.

Indeed the book includes an interview, anonymously given by A.E., the visionary George Russell, whose book *The Candle of Vision* is one of the great classics of modern esoteric mysticism. In this interview Russell describes his visions of the Celtic Otherworld and its denizens, shining and opalescent beings that he defines as two types of the Sidhe, whom he encountered principally on the west coast of Ireland, from Donegal to Kerry, a location he considered to be charged with magical power, as were ancient monuments such as Dowth and New Grange.

In addition to this testimony Evans Wentz recorded many traditional stories of changelings, fairy-brides, the death coach, strange lights, water cattle, the fairy dog, processions, battles, dances, antique attire, difference in time, danger of eating fairy food, offerings left out at night, and euphemisms used to denote 'the gentry' or 'the good people' – who might not always be too well disposed towards their human neighbours, and sometimes with good reason.

However, whilst collections of folklore may hold a certain interest, they do not get us very far in terms of personal experience.

Lone journeys to remote areas of the Celtic fringe, where the veil between the worlds may perhaps be particularly thin, is not an option open to most of us, even if, as Kathleen Raine affirms sixty years later, in a foreword to a new edition of Evans Wentz's book, that what he discovered still remained to be experienced by the perceptive traveller.

There is, however, an alternative that is more readily available to all of us, which is to set about thinning our own personal veil that dulls our perceptions of any inner worlds. This is a great deal easier than is often thought, and does not involve the ingestion of hallucinogenic substances, nor the rigorous application of yogic disciplines over long periods of time. It is simply a matter of the right use of the imagination, with the right aims and in the right context.

Experimentation in this direction has for some time been the dedicated work of R.J. Stewart, a Scottish author, musician and composer who was led to his discoveries largely through the ballad traditions that he explored and exploited intensively. As a result he has held many workshops on these traditions, the fruits and methodology of which he has recounted in a number of books, the most relevant to our purpose being *The Living World of Faery* (Gothic Image, Glastonbury, 1995). I can personally vouch for the validity of his approach, in being one of those, amongst many others, who have entered these realms with him (and safely returned!) on various occasions.

He places this line of work at some distance from what generally passes for occultism, as, like William Blake, he sees it as a quest to inspire our own inherent spiritual vision in a poetic and visionary tradition rather than a regime dictated by discarnate spirits. To me this is also, or should be, the aim of occultism – but that is by the way and part of another story – the need to drag occultism kicking by the heels from many of its outmoded 19th and even 20th century conceptions.

Yet the world of Faery, like that of true occultism, is not a realm of subjective fantasy. It is one of heightened shared reality. This means that any initial experience is probably best gained in the context of a group, and in the company of at least one person who knows by experience what is being sought. In more exclusive circles this is known as initiation but need not be the portentous portal reserved for a few that it is often made out to be.

The key to experience of most inner realms is one of belief. That is to say that faery beings (who exist whether we choose to believe in them or not!) are an independent life form, closely linked to the land, not only to specific localities but to the planet as a whole. Therefore awareness of their world is closely attuned to relating to life in the land, and it is significant that two of Stewart's earlier books are entitled *Earth Light* and *Power within the Land*. This applies to the world as a whole as well as to our own particular patch of it, to which the Society of the Inner Light's long standing concern with what is known as the Planetary Being has considerable relevance. The element of faery tradition is also to be found embedded in Arthurian legend, along with associations of the principle of the Sovereignty of the Land, which may well account for the perennial popularity of these much misunderstood legends, which speak to something within us far deeper than the surface levels of physical objectivity.

For ancient tradition within this is very important, which is why Stewart evokes the traditions to be found in old ballads, and in particular that of the 13th century Thomas the Rhymer, who met the Faery Queen (mistaking her at first for the Queen of Heaven), and was led into her realms to emerge with "the tongue that cannot lie" – to wit, the gift of prophecy. Or the evidence of a remarkable Scottish cleric, the Reverend Robert Kirk, who in the 17th century published *The Secret Commonwealth of Elves, Fauns and Fairies* gathered from his parishioners at Aberfoyle and whom local legend believes to have entered that realm himself.

What happens at one of Stewart's workshops? No one is expected to believe anything, no one is psychoanalysed, psychologised, or told in advance what they are expected to see. As a result indeed, some romantic illusions may well be lost, for it is often believers who are most easily disturbed by genuine encounters, for these are unlikely to be a confirmation of their preconceptions – which may be based more on a mixture of fantasy fiction and Victorian sentimentality than inner reality.

Indeed it is the more materialistic or sceptical individuals who sometimes have the clearest encounters, but are also likely to be surprised to find that faery beings are not diminutive creatures but may well be of human or greater size. This diminution in their assumed size is one that began with the early modern era. The whimsy of *Nymphidia* by the Elizabethan poet Michael Drayton is to some extent responsible, which the dramatic genius of Shakespeare served to confirm, at any rate in the literary mind. (Although Oberon, Titania and Puck are hardly cosy individuals to be confused with imaginations of the Victorian nursery, however twee Peaseblossom and Mustardseed might seem!)

This change in popular perception of faery within the civilised world is no coincidence. Indeed it is of some importance, as arguably being a symptom of the breakdown in inner awareness that the past four hundred years of the scientific and technological revolution has brought. The material gain to humankind has been at the cost of considerable ravaging of the Earth and its other denizens, for the assumption that all is usable, exploitable, discardable, is leading to the destruction of the very environment that has brought us into being, to say nothing of our own moral degradation. To lose sight of the Earth as a living creature, to think that we are no part of her, and that she is not within us, is a misconception at the very heart of our ills, that leads to the factory exploitation of animals, experimentation upon them, and where there is not complete rejection, a trivialisation of the concept of any other forms of inner world life.

Thus the doctrine of the Triune Alliance, contained within an 18th century document quoted by Stewart, may well have considerable relevance for us today, for it renders the recognition of the world of faery not as the idle curiosity of a feckless or superstitious minority but as an urgent need and necessity for our mutual survival, along with a sense of responsibility towards the animal kingdoms.

According to this doctrine, three orders of being live within the world: the human, the faery and the creatures of land and sea and air. The faery races, of which there are many in each land, are of an original perfect unmanifest world; the many species of creatures, which appeared next, are of a manifest and less perfect world; whilst human races, who appeared last, are of a potentially balanced world, to be discovered and realised through knowledge.

All three orders are of one another, but because we do not realise and act upon it, we cause suffering to ourselves and others through our ignorance. The balanced world of humanity should be able to cross back and forth across the threshold of the others at will, and when the unity of the three orders of being is realised then the Sleeper in the Land will awaken.

The identity of the Sleeper has many versions in many traditions, from Merlin the magician, through the wounded King Arthur, to a number of semi-historical characters, or in the wisdom of fairy tales in Snow White and the Sleeping Beauty. In more esoteric circles it refers to the transformation of the Earth from being a 'dark' to a sacred planet, or in traditional Biblical terms it is the coming of the New Jerusalem or the "awake, awake, my love" of the Song of Solomon. A Gnostically derived belief, one that relates to a legend of the Holy Grail being a jewel fallen from Lucifer's crown, would identify the Sleeper at the Heart of the World with the fallen Angel, whose fall was not a spiritual rebellion through pride but a Promethean act of mercy and compassion to the formless Earth at the beginnings of time. In this reading, the imprisoned Lord of this World awaits redemption through the reunification of the three orders of being that inhabit the Earth. It is then that the Light of the Earth may shine back to the Sun, which is its sibling, each knowing that they are united in being and spiritually of the Company of the Stars.

So much for the cosmic or metaphysical implications, but what of the practical means, here and now, whereby it may be accomplished?

It is creative and repeated work with traditional imagery, narratives and visualisations that awaken and realign the energies. More complex methods are to be found in ritual pattern-making and movement. But after the first awakening has occurred, or the faery initiation, the more direct techniques, including individual meditation, can be used at will.

The potent force of the imagination frees up our energy patterns, and gives us a framework of images that hold great potential for inner transformation, for we literally image what we are. And it is only through a culture of organised greed, indifference to others, and materialistic blindness, that we have imaged ourselves into antagonistic isolation, rejecting other orders of life and feeling alone and unloved in the universe. Yet if we used our imaginations to open ourselves up to the potential glory that surrounds us, we might discover this sense of isolation to be an illusion, and find ourselves in world of many beings, and of many realities.

If we work with the light and power within the land, which is our very substance, renewed daily in the food we eat and air we breath, and open ourselves to the energies inherent in the Otherworld, of which the faery realm is the closest to us, then remarkable changes can occur.

The faery realm is the Primal Land, wherever we might be. It is the image of that land before and beyond pollution and corruption, which is the reason for its various names as Land of the Heart's Desire or of the Ever Young. Seemingly the two images, the inner or primal land, and the outer or manifest land, were once closer together, for in a vast range of myths, legends, folk tales and ballads, humans and faery people once intermingled freely, even married, but in time the two worlds parted.

The proper place for encounters with the faery realm nowadays is through the attuned imagination, dedicated to beneficial purposes, with no ulterior or selfish motive. Indeed if our motives are not pure then our experience is likely to be repaid in kind. That is, likely to be educative but not entirely pleasant, for whatever is found within one world has its direct reflection in the other. Thus deceit breeds deceit, faery gold turns to ashes or dead leaves, escapism leads to delusion, sexual adventuring leads to isolation. The faery world is not an idyllic stereotype but has its own energies, cycles, challenges, tests and tasks.

If we desire to enter the faery realm with the aim of bringing back with us the power of a purified and light-filled primal land by which to transform ourselves and our corrupted world, then we are in a good position to meet whatever challenges, tests or tasks may arise. This linking and reawakening brings the realisation that the land about us has inner dimensions of energy and consciousness, and that neither we nor the planet upon which we live is confined to its physical appearance. And as we become attuned to the worlds within, so we may find the companionship of beings known to ancient tradition whose light transforms and regenerates and can bring changes to us on very deep levels, both individually and collectively.

Mind you, this is a far cry from Peter Pan and Tinkerbell, but even these chimera of Edwardian whimsy continue to provide a glimmer of faery tradition and witness to the power of imagination, even into the cynical and war-weary 21st century. And maybe it is not Tinkerbell's fate that is at stake – but our own!

DION FORTUNE AND THE MYSTICAL QABALAH

English text of introduction to the German edition of The Mystical Qabalah,
"Die Mystische Kabbala", Edition Aurinia, Hamburg

I F, AS many people feel, Dion Fortune is one of the key figures in modern occultism within the English speaking world, and founder of one of its most influential schools, this is in no small measure due to her lucid book on the Qabalah. This system of Jewish Hermeticism has been the backbone of European esoteric thought since at least the Renaissance, and formed an underground oral tradition for centuries before it was ever written down. Unfortunately, whatever its importance in the philosophical assumptions of European magi from Raymond Lull to Eliphas Lévi it had never been accorded a treatment that made it readily accessible to the non-specialist enquirer and seeker for occult wisdom.

True, there had been a handful of nineteenth century scholarly treatises and privately published monographs at the turn of the century but it was not until the nineteen thirties that the wondrous potential of the Tree of Life – the central all-embracing symbol of Qabalistic exegesis – was laid before the general public. Dion Fortune laboured at this over a four year period via her own personal meditations, writing up the results as a series of articles in *The Inner Light Magazine* from 1931 to 1934. After being published in volume form in 1935 as *The Mystical Qabalah*, the work has never been out of print, and is now well on the way to providing enlightenment and instruction to another generation of esoteric students.

When she commenced her book Dion Fortune had been actively engaged in practical occult work for nigh on fifteen years. Abandoning a career in psychotherapy upon her realisation that conventional psychology could not account for many of the phenomena of the human mind, she read and studied widely; not only contemporary Theosophy but the trance work and ritual co-masonry of her first teacher, Dr Theodore Moriarty, and the system founded by the Hermetic Order of the Golden Dawn, an off-shoot from the German Rosicrucian tradition. She went on to form her own small group in 1922, which by 1927 had grown sufficiently to become the beginnings of an esoteric school in its own right, the Fraternity of the Inner Light. It was the challenge of this expansion in her role from student to teacher, from group leader to founder of a school, that brought about her commitment to exploring the principles of the Tree of Life through her own processes of discovery by meditation and vision.

First and foremost was her realisation, based upon her practical experience, that the West had its own system of esoteric development that needed no instruction from the East. This is in no sense to deny the importance of the great systems of spiritual teaching embraced by esoteric Hinduism or Buddhism, much of which had been popularised in the west by Madame Blavatsky's Theosophical Society; but although fragmented and even decimated by centuries of religious persecution and latterly by materialistic philosophy, there was nonetheless an indigenous western esoteric tradition that can be recovered with very great profit, for it has the advantage of being well suited to the western form of temperament and life style. Hence her first chapter begins with the claim that what she is about to reveal constitutes nothing less than "the yoga of the west" – as opposed to the idea of many practitioners of the day who sought to provide eastern systems of yoga, adapted for the west.

Having established this point she goes on to point out that her own approach to the Qabalah differs, as far as she knows, from all other writers she has read upon the subject, because for her "it is a living system of spiritual development, not an historical curiosity."

This was brought home to her very vividly in a series of spontaneous visions that came to her as she started to work with the Tree of Life in a practical and systematic way. Although she knew the basic principles of the Tree of Life and the Golden Dawn system of correspondences to it, since her initiation into that group in 1919, she felt that she had been unable to make the most of it because of the demands upon her time and energies brought about by founding the Fraternity of the Inner Light. The time had now come for her to revise and activate her knowledge of the Tree of Life and its intricate system of symbols.

She did this, and much the same process can be followed by any interested student, by reciting to herself each morning the primary correspondences of its ten spheres – particularly the Names of God, the Archangels, the Choirs of Angels and the Planetary Spheres which are to be found listed out in the chapter headings to her book. Then, having established her grasp of the general structure of the system by these means, she began to concentrate upon each sphere in turn, until one day she was startled to find a marked changed in consciousness coming upon her. As she noted at the time:

> I would be sitting in my accustomed chair, conscious of the sounds of the house, the touch of my clothes on my limbs, and all that makes up the sum total of impressions that keep us in touch with the external world when the eyes are closed. Then I would commence my mental rehearsal of the sacred names, and would suddenly find that I was aware of mental pictures only, to the entire exclusion of physical sense impressions. Nevertheless I retained full co-ordination of consciousness, for I knew that I was conscious of the pictures, and that the physical impressions would return unless I maintained my concentration on the images arising in consciousness, and did not allow it to wander.

This method, which is by no means odd or weird or dangerous, is a natural use of the creative imagination which is the prerogative of every normal human being, and one that is so simple that it can be in danger of being overlooked. As the Rosicrucian alchemists used to say, their secret stone is everywhere available but is simply disregarded. For the secret of this "first matter" or *prima materia* we need look no further than the informed and perfectly natural use – and appreciation – of the human imagination, informed and eventually inflamed by its own spiritual source.

And so she continued, covering each of the spheres of the Tree of Life in turn, conscious of the power of her own imagination, and attentive to the kaleidoscope of mental pictures that they brought to her as she sat deep in meditation. The intellectual fruits of her meditations form the gist of the text of her book, although at the time she did not describe her practical method except to students and members of her school. This was not in any sense of exclusiveness but from respect to the tradition of occult secrecy that still existed strongly in her generation. With the long history of persecution visited upon such studies in the west the origins of such secrecy need not be surprising, although beyond sensible measures of discretion and discrimination such caution has now been relaxed for some considerable time. The only secrecy lauded nowadays tends to be on the part of those who know little but wish to hint that they might know much.

The consequence is that whilst the chapters of *The Mystical Qabalah* provide a system of gateways to higher consciousness that can be appreciated at an intellectual level, the key by which to unlock those gates requires the application of the active imagination. It is not difficult nowadays to find elementary instruction in simple techniques of using the imagination to open up various degrees of psychic awareness, but the casual student may well end up wandering, devoid of guidance or direction, in a labyrinth of subconscious imagery without the context of a formal structure such as the Tree of Life. It is here that a text such as *The Mystical Qabalah* is so valuable, in that it provides the much needed guidance.

In general terms the structure is relatively simple. It applies to the universe at large and also to the human frame of consciousness, for both are based upon the same cosmic principles. Thus we have the means of coming to a personal appreciation of the inner kingdoms of both God and man. In the Tree of Life a route map is provided for a great journey or quest that mirrors the history of human consciousness, from spiritual spark of divine fire, down through divine wisdom and understanding to the dynamics of the higher self, into the projected world of material and physical experience, and thence back up through the spheres of higher consciousness to the illumination of the divine light of the spirit.

In diagrammatic terms this can be represented by a simple scheme of three triangles, one for the spiritual world, another for the higher soul or moral world, and one for the psychological world of the everyday personality, from which depends a fourth single sphere representing the physical body and its etheric counterpart. All of this is held within the embrace of a surrounding system of three cosmic Veils behind which is the noumenous reality of the Eternal. All this is in accord with traditional esoteric philosophy in its various historical manifestations, whether Christian gnosis, Greek neoplatonism, or Hermetic tradition, down to the present, illuminated and simplified in the Tree of Life by its clear chart of progress and development, as profound as it is simple.

One of the practical methods of development that can be derived from the Tree of Life is to build symbolic structures inspired by each of its spheres. Indeed Dion Fortune found this to be happening spontaneously, as she records in one of her early experiences, as she sat in front of a coloured picture of the Tree of Life.

Passing in meditation down the spheres and reciting the divine and angelic names, when she came to the ninth one, the purple sphere of Yesod (sacred to the Archangel of the Anunciation, Gabriel, and to the Moon) she found a picture spontaneously forming in her mind. At first it was as if she were looking at it through a window, and then as if she stood in the midst of the scene. It was a sandy desert by moonlight, and at her feet a lake or inland sea rippled against the sand, whilst a few scattered palm trees could be discerned a little behind her, and in the middle distance a string of camels was to be seen slowly moving away. The longer she gazed at the scene the more its sense of reality grew, until she could

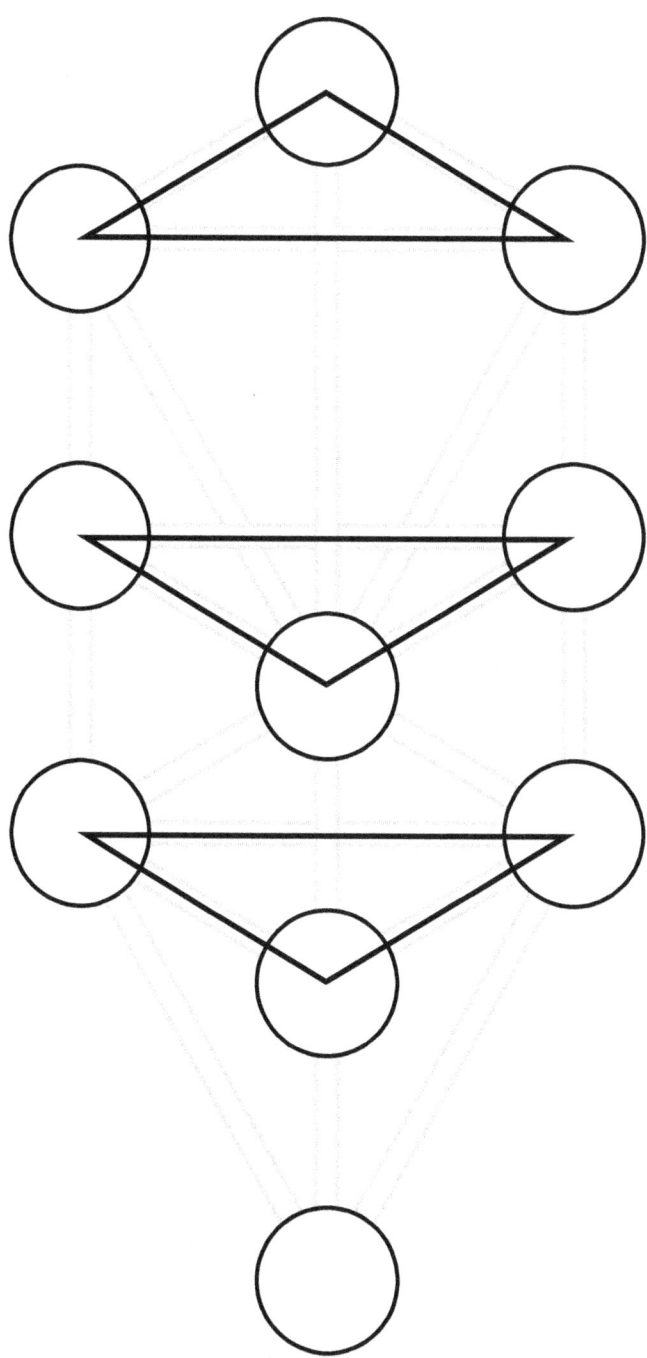

hear the wash of the water as it lapped the sand and see the flash of moonlight upon the ripples, whilst on the horizon, across the water, she could see the white walls of a city, dominated by round white domes.

Then, as she watched, a change occurred. A vast angelic figure began to form in the sky above, bending over her in a vast crescent shaped curve of moonlight greys and misty mauves and blues. Its face was calm and still and very intent as it leaned towards her, and showed her the symbol of a slender cone of white plaster, point upwards, that she felt was in some way associated with the round white domes of the distant city and to be made of the same material.

She makes no further comment about this symbol or its significance, but it is interesting to note that in Egyptian hieroglyphs the cone and dome in juxtaposition indicate the star Sirius, sacred to Isis, whose rising announced the inundation of the Nile and the return of growth and fertility to the land.

The vision persisted until the time came to draw her meditation to a close, at which point, to her astonishment, the purple disc on the chart of the Tree of Life before her seemed to detach itself, expand in size and enter into her aura. Here it seemed to slide right inside her physical body till it took up a position resting upon the floor of her pelvis, just in front of the spine and reaching upwards to the level of the lower ribs, a disc of quivering purple light. She felt that she had in some way been initiated at an unconscious level into some of the mysteries of this realm of the Tree, which represents, amongst other things, the subconscious mind in man, and in the objective world the *anima mundi* or soul of the world. It is not without significance that soon after completing her work upon the Tree of Life as a whole she felt inspired to embark on a spate of creative writing in a series of novels, culminating in *The Sea Priestess* and *Moon Magic*, which are full of the evocation of the symbolism of Yesod – particularly relating to the inner powers of the sea and of the moon and the goddess Isis.

Yesod is but one of the ten spheres of the Tree of Life, and one that lies closest to the realms of material experience and the collective unconscious, just as the higher spheres relate to higher realms of mystical experience. Thus in a later vision she found herself swooping and soaring like a bird before finding herself seated in a white robe and striped head dress seated on a stone block within a temple. Then the whole block seemed to rise up, taking her with it, through the roof and through the clouds and past the indigo vault of the Moon sphere of Yesod, then on into the bright sunlight of the golden sphere of Tiphareth that lies above it – the realm of higher consciousness which in Jungian terms is sometimes referred to as that of the integrated Self, or the Divine Child. Then she continued to rise with breathless rapidity until she entered a great sphere of blinding white light. Here she was no longer conscious of having any bodily form but seemed to be a pure unit of consciousness. She looked down the Tree of Life, whose summit she had reached, and found that she had taken on a form of enormous size, a towering cosmic figure with feet planted on the bluish globe of the Earth seen through clouds. There was a feeling of tremendous force pouring like water from the palms of her hands, her solar plexus and her forehead, which rained down upon the altar below in diamond sparkles of light.

In this experience she felt that she had touched at least the outer levels of her innermost spiritual self, close to the sphere of Kether, the Crown of Creation that in the eastern systems of yoga might be equated with the sahasrara chakra, for the spheres and crossings of the paths of power between the spheres of the Tree of Life up its central pillar have their correspondence with the spinal column and its auric equivalent along with the other yogic chakras. Thus we may see the validity of Dion Fortune's claim for the Qabalah to be 'the yoga of the West'. It is, moreover, a system in its own right, not derived from any eastern source. Nonetheless the systems of east and west do reflect each other, for both describe and approach the same interior reality.

The beauty of the Tree of Life lies in the number of ways in which it can be used as a tool for psychic and spiritual development. For it may be approached upon any of the four principal levels of consciousness. To the God-intoxicated rabbis who formulated the system, each sphere was first and foremost a means of approaching God. God had revealed himself in ten specific ways, each represented by one of the spheres of the Tree, and thus to contemplate any sphere in a pious and reverent way, concentrating upon the particular holy name or names of God associated with it, was a way to high mystical colloquy with the divine.

Or, we can approach it at the philosophical level, which is broadly the way that the text of Dion Fortune's *The Mystical Qabalah* reads, upon the level of the conscious intellectual mind. This is the most convenient way of introduction for most readers, and a level which, once mastered, can be used as a springboard for other levels of working, be it the higher mystical contemplation, or the colourful world of images – commonly called the astral – that Dion Fortune discovered in the meditations we have described. Or, at the more physical level, its symbolism can be utilised for the purposes of fashioning talismans for particular qualities, for constructing rituals of white magic, or as an aid to interpreting astrological charts.

Whichever way we choose to approach the Tree of Life of the Qabalah is a matter for ourselves and own experience and judgement. What Dion Fortune has done is to present to us, in a simple and straightforward way, a general ground plan of the human soul and of the universe. She has provided the map, and now it is up to us, who choose to read her, to follow it.

But no matter how clear her guidance, it is all for nothing if we fail to follow the way she has shown. And so with due humility and dedication, let us take the first step on the way that leads to the inner light.

IS THERE A PSYCHIC IN THE HOUSE?

THERE IS an old saying "Give a dog a bad name and you'll hang it." Much the same could be said about certain occult techniques and none more so than psychism. Indeed there was one period in the Society's history when the current leadership actively tried to dissociate themselves from the subject.

One result of this was to find in the front of new editions of Dion Fortune's books a somewhat patronising notice to the effect that "the works of the late Dion Fortune were written a long time ago and since then a great deal more has been understood and realised so that many of the ideas then expressed are not now necessarily acceptable. Also, much of what she wrote was written from the viewpoint of the psychic."

Too bad that Dion Fortune did not know any better, this seemed to imply, and it is a pity that anyone is still interested in her teaching, which is now outmoded in light of new revelations gained by other means, far superior to the somewhat demimondaine world of psychism in which she was prone to dabble.

Actually things were somewhat more complicated than this. Some elements of esoteric custom and practice were no doubt due for change, particularly concerning the spurious glamours sometimes associated with the grade system of esoteric organisation. Nonetheless, to blame much of this upon psychics and psychism suggests a classic case of Dion Fortune's favourite saying about throwing out the baby with the bath water.

During her lifetime Dion Fortune not only practised psychism but she thought hard and long about it, and its strengths and its weaknesses at its various levels. This she revealed in a number of articles in *The Inner Light Magazine* during the 1930s, and she went into overdrive in 1942 with a series of articles in the pages of the Spiritualist journal *Light*. Much of this has since been republished in *Spiritualism and Occultism*, and her article on *The Rationale of Psychism*, written for the September 1928 issue of *The Occult Review* is another example of her writings upon this theme.

At her death in January 1946 the Society found itself in sudden crisis as she had been the principal channel within the organisation for psychic communication. No-one else had shown anything like her ability and most had been content to leave things as such, not expecting her early demise. Fortunately Margaret Lumley Brown was able to step into the breach and continued to serve in this capacity. A team of supporting workers of varying degrees of aptitude was also developed, serving the archives of the Fraternity well for another fifteen years.

Psychism, like any other occult technique, is not foolproof, particularly in the context of the high inner power levels that can build up within an esoteric fraternity. Consequently, after a particular crisis in 1960, psychism fell out of favour. The leading psychics were more or less pensioned off and the Fraternity took a new direction, more or less in accord with the religious aspirations of the current Warden, who henceforth became known as its Spiritual Director. These remedial measures, at first announced as temporary over a three year transitional period, then acquired an aspect of permanence, and the magical effectiveness and reputation of the Society went into a slow but inexorable decline. This is demonstrable from the archival evidence of the quality of communication received after that date compared with that which went before.

The Society continued to function well enough as a species of well intentioned ethical and religious group, with an interest in Qabalistic philosophy, but otherwise eschewed any association with psychism or the occult tradition, despite the high reputation of its founder along these lines.

A technique known as 'mediation' was encouraged in all members as preferable to psychic ability. This certainly had its points as a

Is There a Psychic in the House?

corrective to misunderstandings pertaining to psychic awareness, for psychism had tended to be put on something of a pedestal, along with its more talented practitioners, and the assumption that only the exceptionally gifted were capable of it.

In fact most people are psychic to some degree or another, but may not recognise it in those terms. It all comes down to the faculty of imagination, which is common to all humanity. As Dion Fortune points out in her *Occult Review* article, imagination is the faculty by which we perceive the physical world about us, and by extension it is also that by which we may perceive the equally pervasive non-physical world too. This can happen in pictorial, verbal or intuitive terms. The main task of a teacher or school is to bring esoteric aspirants to realise this fact and put some faith in their own innate abilities, which should develop along with their faith in themselves and the ideals they seek to serve.

So why, one may ask, is psychism accorded such aversion and distrust even by some who dedicated their lives to the esoteric movement? The illiterate, unbalanced or dishonest psychic has of course been a popular butt of criticism throughout the ages, from Ben Jonson's *The Alchemist*, through Robert Browning's Mr. Sludge the Medium, to Noel Coward's hilarious caricature of Madame Arcati in *Blithe Spirit*. The movement provides some easy targets. The occultist W.G.Gray had a highly amusing party piece, mimicking the medium at a local spiritualist circle who claimed to be the mouthpiece for Queen Victoria, "returned to survey her realm".

Many such examples of inferior psychism give the subject a bad name. However one could say much the same about poetry, water colour sketching, or playing the guitar, but that is no reason to try to ban such pastimes.

The ignorant and unprivileged are of course prone to be deceived by the cheap imitation of real esoteric knowledge and power, for it feeds upon their vulnerability. Conversely, the well educated tend not to be in the forefront of the ranks of psychic practitioners.

In her 1928 article Dion Fortune put her finger upon this very problem. Whilst a well stocked mind is essential for psychic performance of high quality, the formal education that usually goes with developing such a well stocked mind can prove to be a barrier. Knowledge is often achieved at the cost of loss of freedom from intellectual constraints, preconceptions and associations that accord with current academic fashions and assumptions. This can be very insidious and may inhibit much natural psychical ability, much as the shades of the prison house close about the growing child.

The esoteric world is thus an area where the encyclopaedic, promiscuous and often haphazard reading of the voraciously self educated can be a positive advantage. Certainly the best psychics seem to come within this category, not least Dion Fortune and Margaret Lumley Brown. Indeed a lack of formal educational opportunities in the past might well have been a contributing factor to the predominant success of women in the psychic field. Certainly in my own experience I have found it a distinct advantage to come to formal higher education somewhat late in life.

However it is also true that a mind that is not well stocked, culturally, historically and scientifically, whilst free from intellectual inhibitions, is unlikely to be able to produce more than vague generalities and pious maxims. Any likely communicator, of whatever cosmic rank, will be in much the same frustrating position as a typist trying to operate a machine that has lost half its keys.

Exceptions exist, it is true, and evidence that at a certain level of consciousness, everything seen or heard is recorded and can be accessed, to the point that otherwise illiterate persons, even children, have been known to come forth in trance with remarkable displays of erudition. There is also, as has been proved again and again, the fact that psychics may pick up on the pooled subconscious resources of those who are present at the time. This is apparent even with Dion Fortune, as a close reading of *Dion Fortune and the Inner Light* may reveal; in particular, her ability to be a link with the one she called the Master of Medicine varied qualitatively with the personal sympathy and medical knowledge of those with whom she was working, her best work being done with her husband Dr. Thomas Penry Evans.

Is There a Psychic in the House?

Therefore, as she herself observes, in a masterpiece of understatement, an adequate study of the psychology of psychism is subject matter for a book. Indeed it would need to be a very substantial volume too. A number of books have been attempted along these lines, although perhaps not sufficient attention has been paid to what actual intelligent practitioners have had to say about the way they work.

There are also different types of psychism, in practice and intention, and the type that both Dion Fortune and Margaret Lumley Brown aimed for was what they sometimes called cosmic mediumship, as opposed to the general kind of clairvoyance purveyed in spiritualist circles or at psychic fairs.

It should be noted that Dion Fortune takes great pains to distinguish between what she calls on the one hand the trained occultist, and on the other the untrained psychic. The former should have undergone a considerable training in the practice of building images in the imagination as a means of maintaining adequate bearings in the world of the unseen, along with the flexibility and sensitivity to allow other images to rise within these set symbolic pieces. Extending from this can come verbal and intuitive impressions to add greater dimensionality to the experience.

Whilst much can be done by the five finger exercises of private meditation, the greatest aid to development is undoubtedly, where it is available, participation in group work of a structured ceremonial nature. This is analogous to the difference between singing in the bath at home and taking part in a choral ensemble in the company of talented and like-minded friends. In the occult context, telepathic influences within a heightened atmosphere of mutual intention and aspiration can have a powerful influence upon personal psychic development at all levels. Or, in more technical terms, it is a safe and natural development of the etheric centres, which are the avenue for all incoming impressions from the unseen, whether registering as spiritual intuitions via the head, verbal communications through the throat, pictorial associations via the heart and solar plexus, or physical vitality through the lower centres.

Having said this, as with singing so with psychism, some will have greater natural talent than others. Not all can stand forth and commit themselves as soloists, any more than all can be channels for deep and informative esoteric teaching. In a well conducted choir or esoteric society there should be a suitable and fulfilling place for all. And by analogy any self-respecting choir would not consider itself much good if it was unable to muster at least one decent soloist. Similarly in the esoteric equivalent, a group deprived of psychics of superior quality will hardly be distinguished in inner or outer performance.

This can be exacerbated if no adequate line of conscious communication is maintained between the inner and outer echelons of the group soul and mind of an esoteric fraternity. In fact such a group, by Dion Fortune's own terms, will be in danger of losing its contacts. Unless of course those contacts, having once been firmly established, are able to maintain some kind of subliminal link, perhaps through a physical building or corpus of writing, until by some means, in a succeeding generation, the psychic links can be fanned into creative fire again from the ashes of formal convention. A living tradition, like a fire, is an ever changing condition of progressive transformation. A dead one relies on the repetition of former custom and practice without understanding the reasons why. Revelation has given place to precedent.

Although I am no advocate of grandiose titles, occultism having suffered enough from a surfeit of High Priests, High Priestesses and similar Grand Panjandrums of the Self-Regarding Elite, there is much to be said for the maintenance of the office of Pythoness – which need not necessarily rest in single hands. Some of the deeper issues involved were indeed covered by Margaret Lumley Brown in an article, originally a psychic communication, entitled *The Pythian Power*.*

A careful study of this article lays bare a number of important issues. One is the much neglected 'underworld' aspect of psychic communication. That is to say its roots lie within the Earth itself, or

---

* It is reproduced in *Pythoness – the Life and Work of Margaret Lumley Brown* and in an issue of *The Inner Light Journal*, Vernal Equinox 1998.

if one prefers to put it another way, the mode of universal telepathic communication between human beings, incarnate or discarnate, is through the etheric medium, or what has been variously called the World Soul or Anima Mundi.

In other words, one cannot fly directly to Cloud Nine without contacting the inner realms of Earth first. Any attempt to do this results in the disconnected ineffectuality that passes for spirituality in many areas of new age universalism – a kind of high flown subjectivism. Perhaps the most effective counter to this tendency has been expressed in the works of R. J. Stewart, of which *The Underworld Initiation*, *Earth Light* and *Power Within the Land* are salient examples, closely followed by *The Way of Merlin*.

One is not advocating wholesale conversion to his way of thought but it is one important pole in practical applications of occultism. Just as another pole is an appreciation of the everyday applications of Qabalah, as for example in the teaching and works of Z'ev ben Shimon Halevi (Warren Kenton), modern examples straight from the horse's mouth so to speak. *The Work of the Kabbalist*, *A Kabbalistic Universe* and *The Way of Kabbalah* are examples from his oeuvre.

Whilst we may owe a great deal to Dion Fortune in both these avenues, she finished writing in 1945, and although some of her works have taken some years to see the light of day, the world has moved on in the last half century, and we should be aware that there are some other useful teachings around, complementary to our own work, of which we should not remain in ignorance. There is little point in visualising networks of light and goodwill radiating the globe if we do not design to acknowledge our close ideological neighbours.

There are two paragraphs in Margaret Lumley Brown's communication upon the pythian power that bear repetition. One reveals a past situation within the Fraternity, during the 1950s, from which we might well ask if we have perhaps fallen away. Referring to the ancient world she states:

> There were Sibyls belonging to different places: there were several of these in different parts of the ancient world. The best known is the Delphic oracle. All

these act in different ways, not all in the same way. In a small way we in this Fraternity are, as it were, setting up the same thing, for we are making centres of different kinds in which a Pythoness of a certain type brings through a special sort of message, so that history and prehistory repeat themselves, as is often said.

The fruit of such work remains in various sets of papers still available to members of the Fraternity, bearing the hallmark of different masters, Egyptian, Elemental, Hibernian, Greek. Her concluding paragraph pertains to the future:

In Aquarian days, the communications will be more frequent and more universal and the veil thinner and thinner, and the day will come ... when the last veil may be at last rolled back entirely. For that, and to hasten that, we on the inner planes work day and night without ceasing.

Whether we call it mediation, meditation, psychism, clairvoyance, or just plain hunches, it is towards this that we on the outer planes should surely work day and night without ceasing too!

THE MAGICAL WORLD OF DION FORTUNE

Draw a line from St. Alban's Head on the south coast of England up to the holy island of Lindisfarne in the north east, passing through the great stone circle at Avebury, and another from King Arthur's legendary birth place at Tintagel in Cornwall, across to St. Albans north of London, the old Roman city of Verulamium and place of Britain's first Christian martyr, and that line too will pass through Avebury. So says Mona Wilton, heroine of Dion Fortune's novel *The Goat-Foot God*, to Hugh Paston when he is seeking a suitable site to construct a nature temple dedicated to the great god Pan. Thus the land of Albion (the ancient name for Britain the White Island) is divided up into four quarters of great significance, each having a different approach and response to its legends and traditions, be they Brythonic, Celtic, Saxon or Viking.

What makes Dion Fortune's novel differ from the average fantasy novel is that she fully believed in everything she wrote, and not least that which she wrote under the guise of fiction, for in writing fiction she could speak of things that might seem strange if presented as bare fact. For there is a truth of the imagination, that when coming from sufficient depth of knowledge and conviction is just as valid as any more prosaic speculation.

The proof of this is evident in the fact that her novels written almost 90 years ago are still in print today and much of what she wrote in them has been taken on board by the esoteric world. Leylines are commonplace matters of talk nowadays but Dion

Fortune was a pioneer in making their existence more widely known. She was also very conscious of power points throughout the land, and not least that of Glastonbury which she described as the mystical heart of England and where she first set up a group of like-minded friends in a chalet on the lower slopes of Glastonbury Tor.

Her love of Glastonbury is encapsulated in an imaginative guide she wrote that is also still in print, *Avalon of the Heart,* in which she describes the various strands of legend that not only permeate Glastonbury but filter into the subconscious mind of the nation as a whole as part of its natural heritage. Thus in one sense it forms a part of Camelot, for the bodies of King Arthur and Queen Guinevere, in the time of Richard the Lionheart, were discovered by the monks, buried before the high altar of their abbey. It was also the place of the first Christian church in England, a wattle and daub circular structure that predated the abbey, and that legend equates with the coming of Joseph of Arimathea, who after he had taken possession of the body of Christ from Pontius Pilate, was vouchsafed a vision of the Holy Grail and brought a party of devotees to these islands. He landed at Wearyall Hill, then an island, and struck his staff in the ground where it took root, and can still be seen as the Holy Thorn, flowering every Christmas, an offshoot of which grows within the abbey grounds. Dion Fortune's evocation of the ancient traditions of Glastonbury has inspired another generation of novelists to take up the story, not least the epic tale of Marion Zimmer Bradley's *The Mists of Avalon.*

She also evoked yet more ancient traditions of the west and was well placed to do so, for she spent her childhood years in Somerset. Born in 1890 in Llandudno in North Wales, her family moved to Weston super Mare soon after her birth where they helped to run a hydrotherapeutic establishment near Bath.

What gripped the young Dion Fortune's imagination was Brean Down, a spur of land that stretches out into the Bristol Channel at the point where it faces directly onto the wide Atlantic Ocean, unobstructed by the land masses of Ireland, Wales or the Cornish peninsula. It is now a nature reserve and site of great historical importance, owned by the National Trust, and at its far end, before a line of jagged rocks that jut into the sea is an old fort. Built as a defence against the French in the mid nineteenth century, it was abandoned in 1900 although brought back into temporary use during the Second World War.

The fort at the end of the down remains a wild and romantic spot despite the proximity of holiday camps and resorts along the coast, and it is here that the heroine of Dion Fortune's major novel *The Sea Priestess* set up a temple to evoke the powers of the Sea. Her broader aims were to inject by her evocations some of the forgotten ancient powers into the conventional repressive society that she found in the 1930s. At the same time she rebuilt the fractured emotional life of her chosen priest Wilfred Maxwell, transforming him from a limp-wristed wimp, henpecked by his mother and elder sister, into a vibrant and active man, successfully married to a local girl with whom he developed a personal knowledge of the inner worlds revealed to them by the sea priestess.

The psychological side to her work was ever important to Dion Fortune. In her early twenties she had practised as a counsellor at the Medico-Psychological Clinic in London until coming to the conclusion that there was more to the human mind than orthodox psychology was prepared to admit. She came to these conclusions after some unusual experiences of her own. First discovering that she was telepathic when she attended by chance a lecture demonstration on the subject and then after reading Annie Besant's *The Ancient Wisdom*, experiencing a vivid vision where she seemed to be taken up into the high Himalayas to meet two great spiritual beings who set her upon her subsequent life as an esoteric teacher.

At first she learned the ropes through a remarkable occult practitioner, Dr. Theodore Moriarty, and it was watching him at work that first disenchanted her with orthodox psychology. She wrote up some of her experiences of Moriarty at work in a series of short stories published as *The Secrets of Dr. Taverner*, and came close to replicating his work when after Moriarty's death in 1923 she met and married Dr. Thomas Penry Evans with whom she hoped to set up a clinic that combined knowledge and practice of orthodox medicine with the insights of esoteric and spiritual healing. Something of her work on these lines was recently discovered in an exciting literary find and has been published as *Principles of Esoteric Healing*.

Hopes for establishing a clinic were eventually displaced by calls on their time to establish an esoteric school. She had already been initiated into the famous Hermetic Order of the Golden Dawn where she worked under the Scottish novelist John Brodie Innes and Moina MacGregor Mathers, wife of the founder of the Golden Dawn. Nor was the eastern side of things neglected, for she was also a member of the Theosophical Society, becoming President of its Christian Mystic Lodge. However, in 1927 the call came that rather than work with either of these established organisations they should do their own thing. This marked a watershed in her life. Her ideals in starting a school were laid out in two important books, *The Esoteric Orders and their Work* and *The Training and Work of an Initiate* which laid out in modern terms how one might train to become an initiate after the style of the ancient schools of initiation. This was the genesis of the Society of the Inner Light whose work continues strongly to this day.

She followed up with four years' intensive work which resulted in publication of *The Mystical Qabalah*, regarded by many as the most lucid and student friendly introduction to the Tree of Life, the great symbol system that forms the backbone of much of the western esoteric tradition. Then as a means of illustrating some of its metaphysical principles she set about writing a series of novels to show their possible application in daily life.

The first of these was *The Winged Bull*, followed by *The Goat-foot God* and *The Sea Priestess* and finally *Moon Magic*. This last novel is perhaps the most practical of her books, giving very full details of how the Sea Priestess goes about her magical work in the city of London, on the south bank of the Thames, as she teaches her chosen priest the methods and rationale of her work.

Much of the theory and practice in her novels illustrates what she later came to call "the lost secrets of the West". This is an amalgam of orthodox and less orthodox psychological practice. She was very much aware of the latest developments in analytical psychology, being in close correspondence with the Jungian Foundation in Zurich, and from her earlier psychological work she was aware of the importance of techniques of induced autosuggestion, whilst at the same time she became a confidant of a London University academic researching into techniques of Yoga.

Practical examples abound in the relationship between her main characters of the interchange of etheric magnetism, techniques which fell out of fashion in the English speaking world in the mid-nineteenth century, but which continued to have a strong following by practitioners in France.

In her last years Dion Fortune had to struggle with the problems of working within the restrictions upon publishing and public meetings exercised by the conditions of the Second World War. Not in the least subdued by these difficulties, she ran a widespread meditation group by means of a series of weekly letters, the gist of which have since been published as *The Magical Battle of Britain* and, written in the heat of the London blitz, found a new lease of life in bringing comfort and instruction to the victims of 9/11 in New York.

The work of this meditation group brought about deeper concern with the Arthurian legends and the Holy Grail and the possibility of launching a complete training system in three degrees, consisting of the grade of Arthur, concerned with civilised ideals and chivalry, the grade of Merlin, concerned with an awareness of the inner planes and particularly ancient nature and faery contacts, and the grade of Guinevere, concerned with the powers of the human aura and their polar use. Finally there come the high mystical contacts of the Holy Grail. Much of this work sustained the work of the Society of the Inner Light immediately after the war and the gist of it has subsequently been written up by me and published as *The Secret Tradition in Arthurian Legend*.

Another important plank in Dion Fortune's platform in the latter days concerned thoughts about postwar reconstruction, envisaging a world where the forces of materialism might hold unfettered sway. She therefore sought a broad popular front between the esoteric world and the broader spiritualist movement. She herself had, since 1922, developed her own mediumistic capacities which informed much of her work throughout the rest of her life. Because of their occasional abuse, such techniques have been frowned upon in esoteric circles and she had kept this ability secret from all but her immediate colleagues.

Channelling in various forms has now become a widely accepted phenomenon. Dion Fortune had much experience of it, which as a psychologist she was well able to describe uniquely from personal experience. Scattered in many unpublished as well as difficult to obtain published sources, her writings on this have now been collected under the title *Spiritualism and Occultism,* to give perhaps the most lucid account yet in occult or spiritualist literature of the dynamics and techniques of psychic perception and verbal communication.

Dion Fortune died in January 1946 and her body is buried in the municipal cemetery at Glastonbury. Close by is that of her colleague Charles Thomas Loveday, advocate of the Church of the Grail. The work that she began lives on, not only in the Society she founded but in the inspiration of her life. The fact came home very vividly to me when trawling through the archives of the Society to prepare her biography *Dion Fortune and the Inner Light,* a project which turned out to be one of the most educative and rewarding experiences of my own life and one which I feel privileged to have been able to share with others.

THE RED ROSE AND THE WHITE

IN THE legends of Merlin, the young sage discovered two dragons fighting at the base of Vortigern's tower, one red and one white, which was one reason why the tower and the kingdom could not stand. The red dragon still figures on the banner of the Principality of Wales, yet whilst at one level the dragons may have represented conflict between Celt and Saxon, their meaning extends far beyond that.

Later, when Norman French domination had ridden roughshod over the ancient differences in culture and in blood, the emblems of the red rose and the white became the emblems of the rival houses of Lancaster and York. Yet important as conflict in historical circumstance may seem, not least to those who are caught up in it within their own space and time, there is a far deeper archetypal principle at work in the supposed conflict between the red powers and the white.

Indeed the assumption of conflict of opposites might be better described as the interaction of complementary powers. We might also ponder why, in the early legends, the red and the white should be expressed in terms of dragons, and in later times in the form of roses.

Dragon power is a concept that has its roots in two fundamental sources. One is to be seen in the night sky in the constellation of the Dragon that coils about the Pole Star, and that in the course of precession of the equinoxes, caused by the varying tilt of the axis of the Earth, provides pole stars of its own in different ages. Indeed it provides the current one, if we take into account that Ursa Minor, in which Polaris stands, was once regarded as a wing of the Dragon.

At the base of this axial shaft is the Earth itself, whose spinning provides the spectacle of the turning of the heavens for those of us who live upon its surface. And within the Earth what is commonly known as the Dragon power is the root of many subtle energies, and indeed many not so subtle, as in the phenomena of earthquakes and volcanoes.

It is possible to see these two forms of Dragon power in symbolic equilibrium in the Caduceus of Hermes, where they take the part of the two serpents in this great glyph of universal healing, together with the wings, which in ancient depictions of the caduceus may appear near top or bottom of the shaft.

The rose, in contrast to the dragon, gives less of an impression of raw and ancient titanic energies, but more a mature and beautiful expression of life force – the flowering of the dragon power we might say – that shoots up from the roots. "The force that through the green fuse drives the flower" as Dylan Thomas expressed it. And as such the rose appears again and again in human cultural expression.

Dante, in his great high medieval mystical vision, saw a rose floating in eternity as an emblem of heaven itself, each of its petals a human spirit. In the medieval allegory of *The Romance of the Rose* it stood for romantic love. In the seventeenth century Robert Fludd, Thomas Vaughan and the Rosicrucian Brotherhood made it a major symbol in their mystical philosophy. It also played an important role in the Mysteries of Isis in late classical antiquity, as revealed by Apuleius in *The Golden Ass*, as I have been at some pains to describe in *The Rose Cross and the Goddess* and its later American edition *Evoking the Goddess*. After being transformed into an ass by his abuse of the Mysteries, Lucius, the asinine anti-hero, finally found redemption by eating roses borne in procession by a Priest of Isis and went on to become an initiate of Isis and Osiris.

Whilst we would not necessarily advocate eating roses as an esoteric dietary supplement there is much to be said for ingesting its essence by imaginative interaction, and in more recent times it has figured in Dr. Roberto Assegioli's psychosynthesis as a meditation symbol to promote the flowering of spiritual elements in the human psyche.

However there can be more to this powerful symbol than its application to personal psychology. It has a reality of its own as a doorway to objective states beyond the mundane world. This is amply demonstrated in a book by R. J. Stewart, *The Well of Light*.

Subtitled *The Mystery of the Double Rose*, it is the most recent in a series of books that mark his progress as an esoteric teacher and researcher over the past twenty years. They include *The UnderWorld Initiation* (1985), *Earth Light* (1991), *Power Within the Land* (1992), and *The Living World of Faery* (1995), the earliest of which, as he generously acknowledges, was road tested at some pioneering workshops of mine at Hawkwood College in the early 1980s.

The rose is seen as a focus for objective powers that can be contacted in a form of spiritual healing drawn from folklore tradition that involves a working relationship between humans and the spiritual forces of the land or region in which they live. In the larger context, it can become a form of Earth healing, a way of healing the wounded relationship between humanity and the planet. In more personal application it provides a way of identifying and developing one's own particular aptitudes for this kind of work.

Supplemented by a compact disc, the book contains a series of meditations, visions and ceremonies, not least of which is that of the Well of Light of the title. This is located at the conjunction of the six directions of inner space, four leading to and from the cardinal points, the source points of the four Elements, together with the Above and the Below, which may well be equated with the Dragon powers already mentioned. Sited within a low dry stone wall at the centre of a crossroads, the well shaft links the above and the below, whilst about it are ranged briar hedges of red and white roses. These represent a formidable obstacle but the bushes will part to allow access to the well to whoever is worthy and has taken the trouble to find the key to do so.

Part of this key lies in the significance of each of the five petals of the red or white roses. The petals of the red represent forces that flow through the human body, and systematic working with these spiritual and transformative forces brings self-realisation, including the masculine and feminine sides of oneself and of all humanity going back through time (the ancestors), and relationship to faery allies and companion living creatures of the natural world. The petals of the white rose concern forces that do not flow through the human body until the work of creating the double rose is completed, and these bring deeper forces that include the contact of mediators and teachers, and the 'shining ones' who weave the forces behind form, and ultimately the source of spiritual light at the heart of the Earth itself.

At one end of the ultimate spectrum are the Universal Beings reflected in the stars (called Great Entities or Solar Logoi in the language of *The Cosmic Doctrine*), and at the other the Planetary Being (termed by some schools, or in the first draft of *The Cosmic Doctrine*, the Planetary Spirit). Names however are merely crutches for the limping intellect and can serve to trip us up as easily as support us. As with any Mystery system, what we have to do ultimately is to take a leap of faith and become engaged with it.

This is not necessarily an incitement to take at face value the claims of any self-styled guru or esoteric teacher without evidence of a reasonable track record. However, Stewart's sources have an impressive record in terms of self-preservation and regeneration, for they are rooted in the ballad tradition. As an accomplished composer and performer in the first instance, he found certain traditional ballads to contain ancient mythic themes and very specific magical imagery, that led at a deeper level to secrets of initiation into the faery tradition and the mysteries of the Goddess. Examples from which he quotes include *Tam Lin*, which concerns the triumph of human love over the powers of the Otherworld, and *Thomas the Rhymer* which is about the true understanding the Otherworld mysteries.

As he claims from experience over the years, whilst much esoteric teaching can be woven around this material, spiritual and magical power flows whenever the ballads are sung. What is more, this occurs even though singer or listeners may have little understanding of the meaning behind the words. And this is perhaps why they have survived as vehicles of secret teaching and tradition over the centuries.

Much the same dynamic can be seen in the Tarot as a card game containing a wisdom tradition. Or of the comic erotic novel of Apuleius containing the Mysteries of Isis. When it comes to the survival of an arcanum, it is the power that matters rather than the interpretation. Sooner or later its validity will become self evident when it is really needed. We all recognise light when we see it. The warmth of companionship when we feel it. The wellbeing that comes with harmonised balance. In such perennial images lies the healing of the self and the world – and this is arguably a time when it was never more needed.

www.ingramcontent.com/pod-product-compliance
Lightning Source LLC
Chambersburg PA
CBHW031151160426
43193CB00008B/332